CHANGING COLLARS

Mark Hayden

Changing Collars

the columba press

First published in 2007 by
the columba press
55A Spruce Avenue, Stillorgan Industrial Park,
Blackrock, Co Dublin

Reprinted 2007

Cover by Bill Bolger
Cover photo: www.imagemastersstudio.ie
Origination by The Columba Press
Printed in Ireland by ColourBooks Ltd, Dublin

ISBN 978 1 85607 572 5

Table of Contents

Dedication
To Lorraine, who continues to walk this path with me;
to Luke and Daniel,
who make sense of it all and who make the journey so worthwhile;
to my parents who weathered the storm
and still love me in spite of it all;
to Walton who opened the door and also took a leap of faith;
to those who want to stay but feel they can't
and especially to those who want to leave but can't.

Introduction

This book is the end result of answering the same questions that people have asked me over the last number of years about my decision in the 1990s to resign from the Roman Catholic priesthood and train and commence a life of ministry as a priest of the Church of Ireland.

There is much discussion in the media at the moment about the whole question of priestly celibacy within the Roman Catholic Church. Those who argue in favour of a change in the rule of celibacy point to the fact that there are already married priests serving within the Roman Catholic Church, former Anglican priests who have converted and were re-ordained to serve as Roman Catholic priests. These men have been well received by the parishes in which they serve, and advocates of at least an open dialogue point to this fact as proof of the faithful's readiness for a married clergy.

What many people fail to appreciate is that this is a two-way road. Many Anglican clergy worldwide have left the Anglican Church for one reason or another and have gone on to serve in the Roman Catholic Church. A large number of Roman Catholic clergy have taken the opposite direction and have left the Roman Catholic Church and become priests within the Anglican Church worldwide. I know of a number of such priests serving in Ireland – with three of us serving in the Diocese of Ferns! The good people of Gorey are well used to seeing the local minister walking around town with his young children but it is still a strange sight for many of the visitors during the summer to see a priest pushing a buggy or chasing after his eldest. I sometimes would love to say 'Not everyone in a collar is a Catholic priest' but then in my case perhaps this statement is somewhat confused because I was a Roman Catholic priest. I was never laicised but was informed that I would be excommunicated if I continued with my decision to leave and become an Anglican.

Some people presume that I left just so I could marry. However, as you will read, this is not the case and to be honest, given the difficult world that is priestly ministry today, if my only reason for leaving was for marriage I would not be working as a priest today.

I hope that I have written this book in an open and honest way. If you have bought it in the hope of a tirade against my birth church then I am sorry but you will be disappointed. If you bought it in the hope of a tabloid exposé of the lives of priests and people you may think are referred to within its pages you will also be disappointed. If you want to read a story about someone who made choices that were hard but had to be made, who muddled through for a long time until he couldn't muddle any longer, and who finally took a leap of faith unsure of where it would lead, then read on and I hope you enjoy what I have written.

CHAPTER ONE

Early days

Priesthood had never been on the agenda for me. I was born in 1968 to T. J. and Marie. I grew up in a caring and hardworking home where the work ethic was instilled in me from an early age. We lived in a rural part of County Wicklow between the villages of Kilcoole and Newcastle. In the 1970s this was a quiet area with many farms in full operation and many of the locals working in Bray, Greystones, Dublin and beyond. Many of the young people were working overseas, because work was thin on the ground.

I attended primary school in the local national school in Kilcoole and received and excellent grounding in education from many dedicated staff. One member of staff was clearly unsuited to teach young children and left not long after I moved into First Class and nobody was sad to see her leave, least of all the parents. My teacher for First to Fourth Class and my teacher for Fifth and Sixth Class were wonderful men who instilled a great love of history and language in me and I still count them as friends to this day.

I left primary school in 1981 and as a result was in secondary school during the economic depression of the 1980s. The options for those who stayed on to Leaving Certificate were limited – college if one's family could afford it, state jobs if one was 'connected' or just lucky, a rare job if one was very lucky, emigration the ever present shadow, and the dole for most in the vain hope of a training scheme or a job.

I have always been fascinated with the military way of life and, for me, the one career I desired was in uniform. To this end

I joined the Civil Defence as soon as I was old enough so as to have uniformed experience on my very sparse CV. I loved the varied roles I experienced as a volunteer and knew that a life in uniformed service was for me – little did I know what lay ahead. The Permanent Defence Forces of the Irish Republic in the 1980s were struggling in the face of a recruitment embargo, government indifference and a lack of funding to update equipment and training. It was almost impossible to join the military of my own country so I looked 'across the water' to the British Armed Forces. I was happy to serve in a foreign army but this option evoked a fear in the minds of my parents. This was a time when British soldiers were being killed on a regular basis in Northern Ireland and Southern Irish members of the British Armed Forces could not come home for fear of IRA attack or consequences for their families.

Never being overly concerned at the consequences of going my own way (spoken like a true 18-year-old), I went to stay with my uncle in England in the summer of 1985. He had served in the United States Air Force and was a very good advert for a life in the military. I spent the next week going around the various recruitment offices in Warrington and Liverpool. The British Army seemed very keen for Southern Irish recruits and the Colour Sergeant was very positive about a life in service. The first RAF office I went into was a joke. I was told my educational qualifications were useless, that it was hard for an Irishman to join up, and when I asked the Sergeant about some of the aircraft in the photos on the walls he hadn't a clue about them. Clearly not someone very happy in his job. Undeterred, I went to another RAF recruitment office and met a very nice Flight Sergeant who suggested completing my examinations and returning the following year for officer candidate selection.

I was delighted with this prospect and went home to face reluctance from my father, unhappy at the prospect of his son serving in the RAF. As I have already mentioned, this was a time when Irish people serving in the British armed forces, and indeed their loved ones, were at a very real risk from the republican movement, so his concern was entirely justified and understandable. Funnily enough, it was from around this time on that he suggested priesthood as a career path, albeit with tongue firmly in cheek at first. (Coincidentally, I had also visited a cousin in Liverpool who was a member of a religious order and one of her fellow sisters had remarked what a nice priest I would make – was I getting a sign from the Almighty?) This advice, serious or not, was ironic given that he had never been overtly religious when I was growing up, but had returned to the public practice of his faith when I was a teenager and has been a committed Christian ever since.

When I returned to secondary school in September 1985, the staff began the build up for the Leaving Certificate immediately. There were career nights, preparation of CAO (Central Applications Office) forms for college and the endless questions 'What are you going to do afterwards?' I was quite open that I was going to join the Royal Air Force and nobody batted an eyelid. However, everything was about to change very soon after school resumed in that warm autumn of 1985.

The school I went to for my secondary education is in Greystones, County Wicklow and is called St David's Secondary School. It is a co-educational school under the patronage of the Holy Faith Sisters and during my time there a number of sisters were still teaching in the school. The school always placed a great emphasis on the importance of faith in the curriculum but had a very balanced approach, with non-Catholic pupils being exempted from the religion classes if they wished or fully included if they wished. A new school chaplain was appointed to the school towards the end of my studies there and he was a very popular choice. He was down to earth, dedicated and clearly very happy to be a priest. This was at a time when priesthood and religious life was still viewed as a normal choice for young men and women to pursue. The annual retreat for sixth years always took place in October so as not to interfere with revision schedules closer to exam time. The theme of the retreat that year was vocation and the call to serve others. Whilst not an outright sales pitch for priesthood, the chaplain gave a very honest and interesting account of his life as a priest to date, and his final comments struck a chord deep within me for some reason. He asked us not to dismiss the possibility of religious life as a future way of life and left it at that.

After the retreat I went on with my normal routine: school, study, Civil Defence and weekend work doing the gardening for a retired couple near my home. From time to time the call to priesthood crossed my mind and I dismissed it with amusement at first. I liked women, so why choose a way of life that ruled out relationships? It also seemed a very lonely life with no great permanency, given that priests were moved around every few years. I kept these thoughts very much to myself for a while but it got to the stage that I had to talk to someone about what was becoming a recurring concern in my mind. As I didn't know any of the parish clergy that well, despite being a regular attender at church, I decided to approach the school chaplain and talk out my concerns with him.

I made it my business to bump into the chaplain on the corridor between classes one morning, as I knew he said his prayers walking along the corridors. When I met him I asked him if I could talk to him about something that had been troubling me since the retreat. He arranged a time for me to see him during a religion class, which was the normal time for the chaplain to talk to students on a one-to-one basis. When the time came for the meeting I had convinced myself that I did not have a vocation as I had not experienced any tangible form of calling from God, or so I believed. The school chaplain was very friendly and put me at my ease immediately. I still wonder if he thought I was in some kind of trouble with me asking to see him, but he was completely unfazed when I told him that I thought that I might be considering the priesthood as my way of life. He made no bones about the fact that it was a hard but rewarding life. After quite a long chat, I asked him what was the next step to see if priesthood was really for me.

As the chaplain was a member of a religious order he naturally steered me towards his own order, as the lack of vocations was beginning to be felt by all of the orders. The chaplain advised me to keep my interest in the priesthood to myself for the time being to avoid unnecessary teasing from classmates – good advice as it turned out. In January 1986 I went to a vocations workshop for a religious order based on Dublin's south side. There were about 8 of us on the workshop that ran for a weekend of my Christmas holidays. As far as I can remember, all of the 8 were Leaving Certificate students and we were from all over Ireland, both North and South. We had a number of lectures about what it was like to work as a missionary priest and also on how the order took the place of the priest's family. I found this part daunting as family was very important to me, and still is. The most interesting talks were the informal ones we had with the novices who were in their second year of formation. They told us what it was really like in the novitiate and that conditions were not as good as were being portrayed by those running the weekend. One funny memory I have of that weekend is getting up one morning and trying to open the curtains only to find them frozen to the window!

After the vocations weekend was over I had answered one question but was now faced with another: I did not want to be a member of that religious order, but did that mean I had no vocation? Somewhat nervously I went to the chaplain after the holidays and told him how I was feeling. I didn't want to hurt his feelings but his attitude was admirable – 'naturally I would like to see you in my order but there are plenty of other options – what about the diocese?' I didn't know what he meant so he explained that I could well be being called to be a secular priest – one who serves in his own diocese, which in my case was the Archdiocese of Dublin. The chaplain suggested that I contact one of my parish clergy to be put in touch with the vocations director for the diocese. That evening I rang the Parish Priest – no answer. I rang the local curate – no answer. Then my mother rang the curate in the outlying parish – he was in. My mother told him she wanted to bring her son to see him and his answer was: 'Come on up now – I'll sort him out for you!' I never did find out what he thought I was getting up to, but he answered the door and glared at me until we sat down in his office and he asked me what was wrong? 'Well, Father, I would like to find out about becoming a priest in the diocese.' His face was priceless but, all credit to him, he never missed a beat and got the number of the vocations director for me and said he would phone him so that he could expect a call from me.

Things seemed to go very quickly after that. In February I met the vocations director in Carysfort College and we had a long chat about why I wanted to become a priest and what was involved. In March 1986 I went to Holy Cross College, the diocesan seminary, for the first time to undertake the psychological assessment tests to determine if I was suitable for priesthood. Six of us attended on the day and up until September of that year I thought that this would be my year group, if I were to be accepted for the priesthood. I still wonder at the usefulness of these tests, as I put down what I thought the authorities wanted to hear. The psychologist was very friendly and I subsequently enjoyed the two years of lectures I attended with him in First and Second Philosophy (Second and Third Year). I then had a number of interviews with priests from the college who were sounding me out, as well as two meetings with the president of the college. Many questions were asked during this time but one sticks in my mind: 'Mark, have you ever slept with a man?' 'Eh, no Father.' 'Of course not. Now depending on your exam results we would be happy to consider you for First Year in September.' It didn't seem to matter if I was sleeping with women but the only concern was if I was gay. (This was one of only two times that sexuality was mentioned in the course of my training for the priesthood. The next time would occur towards the end of my training when an *optional* workshop on celibacy was offered.)

So from April 1986 my mind was occupied with the forthcoming exams. I confided in some close friends what my future plans were. Some were incredulous but were supportive in the main. The news leaked after the Easter holidays and I had to endure some teasing but nothing too serious. You must remember that this was well before all the scandals that rocked the Roman Catholic Church in the 1990s.

The exams came and went and the long summer stretched out before me. I continued working at my gardening job whilst wondering how my exam results would go. Most of my classmates were also contemplating what the future held for them. Some had applied for college courses, others had sought out jobs but a large number of the year felt that their futures lay outside of Ireland.

In August the exam results came out and I had achieved enough points to be accepted for seminary training. When I think back on it all now, I marvel at how little I actually knew about what lay ahead for me. I contacted the president of the college informing him of my results and he confirmed my place in the First Year class of 1986. A letter confirming this acceptance followed shortly, along with a list of required items and an entry date of 17 September.

The time between exam results and entry to seminary seemed to go in a blur. I had to go to Dublin for my medical (cursory, to say the least) and to be measured for my soutane – the black robe worn by seminarians and priests – and surplice, buy clerical shirts, black trousers, shoes and so on. I didn't know that I needed a breviary (daily prayer book) but the sisters from St David's Convent kindly bought the 3 volume set for me (a sizeable outlay of money at the time). The school chaplain bought my Sunday and daily missals for me and my father's brothers and sisters made a collection and gave me a large amount of money. I was the first member of our family to go forward to Third Level education so my departure was viewed as quite an event, priesthood aside.

One Saturday afternoon, not long before we entered, the new First Years were invited to the Vocation Director's home for mass and tea. I expected to see the five other people I had completed the psychological assessments with, but to my surprise I walked into a room with fourteen other men. I didn't realise that there were so many of us in the year. I did not know that the assessments were broken up into groups of five or six to make the day easier on those running them. So here we all were. I was one of four school leavers and the others were from all walks of life, mainly from Dublin. I was one of the few 'culchies' from the outlying regions of the diocese and I would soon get used to the slagging as we were a high spirited bunch, to say the least. There was also one other student due to arrive at the beginning of October from the Lebanon. At the time, the Archdiocese of Dublin had links with the Maronite Church in Lebanon and it was the norm for a student to train in Dublin for four years, entering in First year and then skipping on to Senior Theology. Once this student arrived we would number sixteen, the biggest intake in a number of years. That same year fourteen deacons had been ordained to the priesthood. This was to be the last time such a large number of priests were ordained for Dublin.

CHAPTER TWO

Junior House blues

Wednesday 17 September 1986 dawned at last. I had all of what I thought I needed packed and ready to go. The students were due at the college for tea at 7.30pm along with their families, and we all duly arrived more or less at the same time. I was shown to my room at the top of Junior House by the Dean of Students who made me feel very welcome.

I was struck at how bare the room was with its fluorescent lighting, push on taps, linoleum floor and magnolia walls. I could see the Sugar Loaf Mountain from my window and on the other side lay home, so I didn't feel too isolated. (That was to come.) I then was shown down to a room – the Refectory – where I was to eat for the next seven years – the dining hall at Hogwarts it wasn't! I was soon to learn the ways of the Refectory, i.e. don't sit in the middle of a table if you wanted to eat in peace; get down early for warm toast at breakfast and early for chips at tea; don't sit at the deacons' table and remember not to get caught messing during the readings after lunch.

It was a relief when my parents finally left and we returned to our corridor to find lists of books, timetables for college life and the schedule for the next few days until the rest of the students returned from the holidays. This was the first year that the new academic year did not commence with a week long silent retreat. I also learned that we were only going to number fifteen as one of the potential First Years had changed his mind at the last moment and never entered. Our Lebanese classmate never turned up but opted to stay in Lebanon to study, so we remained fourteen for the formation year – the formal title of the first year in Holy Cross College.

I found the first few weeks in seminary very unsettling. This was the first time I had lived away from home, and I had come into a regime that treated us like children – just when I thought I had come to be seen as an adult by society. Up for mass or prayers for 7.30 am, breakfast at 8.15, classes from 9 until lunch time. Lunch at 1pm and then free until 5.45pm to either study, play sport, go into town or whatever one did with one's time. Mass or prayers at 5.45pm followed by tea at 6.30pm. If you were on wash up (a Junior House duty and hated by all) you didn't get out of the Refectory until at least 8pm and then back to studies or pastoral work until bedtime. We, as First Years, were under curfew from 6.30pm unless we were on pastoral work. This meant that we had no permission to be out of the college grounds unless we had a specific reason. This was a regime far harsher than what I had grown up with. The food in general was repetitious and I have never known a place to ruin so much good food and make it tasteless, and yet on feast days a wonderful meal could be produced!

One evening one of the students had managed to obtain a copy of 'The Life of Brian' on video. This Monty Python classic had been banned in Ireland by the censor due to the close similarities with the life of Christ and if we had been found watching it there would have been serious consequences. We ended up watching the video at the farthest end of the college with one of us taking turns to keep watch so that we were not discovered. It was little events like this that managed to keep us sane and also allowed us to maintain a spark of independence in an environment that insisted upon conformity.

My academic studies took place in the Mater Dei Institute of Education for First Year. This was the teacher training college for post primary religion teachers for the Archdiocese, but a course called Formation was also run there for First Year seminarians and brothers and any other religious who wanted a year of studies as a sabbatical year. The student body of Mater Dei was predominantly female and the seminarians were very popular with the ladies of the college, but not with the gents as we were viewed as unfair competition. Forbidden fruit is always sweeter, as they say! I was asked by our class priest – a mentor for the year – if I would consider retaking some Leaving Certificate subjects in order to obtain the extra 2 points to go to University College Dublin to do a degree course, but I was happy to attend the house Philosophy classes for Second and Third Year as I knew there was a chance of completing the theology degree later on in Senior House. This is a decision I have never regretted, but I do wonder if UCD would have led me to question my choices about priesthood sooner. That's one question I will never be able to answer, but a valid question nonetheless.

Pastoral work was part and parcel of the routine for all students. As the seminary was based on the north inner city of Dublin, there was a wealth of opportunities for students. I was placed, along with a classmate, in a St Vincent de Paul Conference working in the inner city and I found the experience eye opening to say the least. The St Vincent de Paul Society provided much needed support to less well off families in the city. I was horrified at the poverty in which many of these people lived and marvelled at the resolve they displayed. My placement in this area was ironic, seeing that a great-uncle of mine had earned quite a good living running a pawn shop on Marlborough Street in the 1940s and 1950s, just around the corner from where I was now working. Heroin had begun to grip this community and it was not uncommon to see used needles and syringes lying on the streets from time to time. I was not street wise in any way but working in this part of town soon cured that. When I would go home on my Thursday afternoon off, I would walk down Jones Road (past Croke Park), down North Circular Road, and into Connolly Station to catch the DART train to Bray. Fine in the day time, but a different prospect at night in the smoggy winters of 1986-88. However, my year as a 'Vincent' around the corner from Summerhill had made me known to many of the youngsters and I can say in all honesty that I walked these streets at all times of the day and night for seven years without any trouble, at a time when the place was rife with drug related crime. It was very much a case that if you tried to help the people of this area, you were afforded a certain degree of protection. Maybe I was just lucky, but I do believe that they left me alone because I was part of the team helping them out.

First Year was difficult because we were all getting to know each other and cliques would from and break up, but I kept very much to myself, sometimes not always by choice. I felt that I was very often on the outside looking in, but still formed friendships with some of my class. I am an only child and must admit to being a classic example of an only child – not good at mixing and very short in the sense of humour department. I found myself on the outside because I found it hard to fit in. I was not used to the constant slagging that went on and very often took a joke seriously and ended up fighting with many of my classmates over some perceived slight or insult which was, in actual fact, just leg pulling. One of my good friends from seminary days used to refer to me as being like a clockwork toy – easy to wind up and set off! This took a long time to change and I had to develop a sense of humour during my time in Clonliffe. I am very glad that I did develop a good sense of humour as I would not have got through the seven years without one.

We were known as the 'water babies' because we blew off steam with water fights, to the extent that we were all interviewed at the end of the year about our behaviour. My main memory from First Year is the late Archbishop Kevin McNamara who was fighting terminal cancer at the time we entered. I was touched that he made the effort of getting out of his sick bed to come and welcome us to the college and we all had great respect for him as a result. His death was a time of sadness for us all and I was honoured to take my turn as part of his guard of honour when he lay in state in the college church. The number of people who came to see him was unbelievable and we were under orders to make sure that no one took anything from his coffin as a memento. Many people put in little notes, prayer cards and flowers, testimony to the affection in which he was held by the faithful. Many 'in the know' were amused at the deep distress displayed by some clergy who were on record as being vehemently against Archbishop McNamara's appointment in the first place. I witnessed the first of many crocodile tears that I was to see over the next seven years and beyond, but many people throughout the Archdiocese were genuinely saddened at the Archbishop's untimely death.

Students had to work in the summer months to support themselves in the following academic year, and in the summer of 1987 I worked as a summer project co-ordinator. A tough job but more important experience of working with people and above all learning when to keep my opinion to myself! I worked on the south side of Dublin and found the task difficult and draining but did enjoy it at the same time. Going back to college was different this time as I knew what to expect and I began Second Year/First Philosophy with the eternal wisdom and arrogance of Second Years the world over! We also began the year with the funeral of the college Spiritual Director, Fr Martin Rafferty CM, a wise and eccentric priest who told me early on that I should leave for a few years and live life a little. How right he was. He died suddenly just before we returned to seminary and I regret not knowing him better, but I still use some of his classic one-liners in sermons!

The Archdiocese also had a new Archbishop, a surprise appointment from the academic world, but the Archbishop did not feature much in the world of a Second Year, except to be greeted respectfully when met in the grounds after meals. Philosophy was a new experience for me – psychology, sociology, ethics,

Egyptology, anthropology, history of art and so on. I did object to having to do English classes as I had obtained a good Leaving Certificate result in English. Oh, the arrogance of youth! We also began the study of homiletics. At first I viewed the lecturer with some reserve but as the years went on I came to value him as one of the most Christian members of staff we had. Ironic that he himself was treated so badly later on in his ministry but has come through it in one piece – a testimony to the strength of the man. Many of the lecturers were from outside of the seminary staff and it was a change to have people from the 'outside' lecture to us. In Second Year I became more involved with the seminary choir and also became a cantor – a soloist – a role which was to continue until I left Clonliffe.

My pastoral placement for this year was a far more daunting prospect as I was assigned, along with two classmates, to a residential centre for special needs young people, and this revealed a deep-seated fear of people with special needs that I was completely unaware of. It is unsettling when you discover a deep fear and prejudice within yourself, but thanks to the care of the head sister and two of the volunteers, I overcame this fear and learned to work happily in this placement. I learned at lot from those ladies and they helped make much of what I am today. For that I am deeply grateful.

Second Year passed quickly, with exams coming and going at Christmas time, and it was in the term after Christmas that three of us decided that we would take up the J1 visa programme on offer for students to work in the United States. We opted to work in the diocesan seminary in New York and, after jobs and visas were secured, we spent the rest of the year saving what dollars we could to keep us going at the start of our journey in the USA.

During this time, one of our classmates disappeared for a while and then returned to college. This was not long after two members of our year left the college, one after the Christmas holidays and one not long after the exams. When a classmate decides that it is time to go, it is very unsettling for the whole class and we presumed that this was why another classmate had taken time out.

Life went back to normal and Second Year drew to a close as the Republic of Ireland football team went off to Germany for the European Cup Final. The Sunday before we went to America, Ireland beat England and the excitement of the time is etched on my memory.

Living and working in New York was quite an experience. I painted rooms in the seminary during the week and cleaned apartments in Manhattan at the weekends. The regime in St Joseph's Seminary was far more strict than what we had at home (believe it or not!) the students staying for the summer language schools were expected to be at mass at 6.15 am every morning, and so were we. So much for holidays in the USA! I had a moustache at this time, or at least what passed for one, and it was a topic of conversation for clergy and students alike, as students of the Archdiocese of New York were not allowed facial hair because it was viewed as vanity. Cardinal O'Connor ran a very tight ship and I remember the opening mass of the academic year which took place not long before we returned home to Ireland. At the mass, the Cardinal informed the student body that he was concerned at the number of students who were seriously overweight and that they would not be ordained until they had lost a considerable amount of weight! Imagine that being a requirement for ordination in these politically correct times.

I took the opportunity of visiting family in Connecticut and California while I was in America, and how much the world has changed since 2001. I travelled across the United States on a ticket in the name of my cousin, who paid for the tickets. The airline I travelled with is no longer in operation, but it was easy to travel anonymously in America before the horrible events of 11

September 2001. I was glad to get back to Ireland as my maternal grandmother had died whilst I was in America and I was glad to spend a few weeks at home before the beginning of Second Philosophy – my third year in seminary.

My year returned to discover that we would be living in Senior House for the coming year – an unheard of event for Junior House students and much to the chagrin of the Pastoral Year students who would normally have moved to Senior House after three years in Junior House. It doesn't sound like much but the rooms in Senior House had turn on taps, a window sill and decent wardrobes – that meant a lot to those of us who lived in the more basic environs of Junior House. There was also the mental step of moving into the senior side of the college – a step closer to ordination.

It is amazing looking back at this time how desperate many of us were to be ordained, just that. The concept of what life afterwards would be like never came into the equation. I have to be very honest here and also say that the college, in my opinion, did not prepare us for the life we would be living as ordained priests. My memory of my formation in Clonliffe is that its aim was to turn out priests who knew how to discuss theology at great length, who knew when to attend lectures and mass and to pray the daily office. I was not taught how to chair meetings, conduct many of the sacraments, how to run a home or how to manage my tax. This may seem trivial but when I was eventually ordained, I was sent out into the diocese with no concept of what I was going to do as a curate, much less how to manage money, bills or even look after myself. Surely within the seven years of formation there could have been time for budgeting, cooking, tax matters and so on. As I will explain later I was not even taught how to give the last rites prior to ordination. The whole emphasis in seminary was focused on *becoming* a priest, not how to live and work as a priest. I will concede that a number of recently ordained priests were invited in to talk to us

when we were students but this took place a good five years before I was ordained. Would we have listened to any priest who
told us the cold hard facts of ministry in the real world? Perhaps
not, but it would have been nice to have been given the option to
decide.

The move into Senior House was great news to us but was
tempered by the news that one of our classmates would not be
rejoining us for Third Year. We had already lost our 'Senior
Man' who skipped two years to join the new Second Theology
class (Fifth Year) and was then shipped off to Maynooth – it had
always been the practice for a Dublin student to complete his
Senior Theology in St Patrick's Maynooth. The Third and Fourth
Years of training in Clonliffe could be deemed optional if a student
was older or already held a degree.

We had known about our classmate's impending departure
for Kildare since May, but we hadn't known anything was going
on with the other member of our class who had failed to return
with the rest of us after the holidays. It seems he was called in to
meet the President during the last weeks of the holidays and 'invited not to return'. Many stories flew around as to why this
happened and it is not for me to repeat any of them here, but in
my opinion it was handled very badly by the college authorities
and our year went around wondering who was next for at least
three months. At no time was any attempt made by the authorities
to speak to the year to allow them to ask what had happened or
to put our minds at rest. The quote from Christ comes to mind:
'Do unto others as you would have them do unto you.'

My pastoral assignment for this year was an utter and complete disaster from my point of view. I was attached to a youth
information office run by a church-based organisation on the
south side of the city. The person in charge viewed me as an unpaid labourer and I was treated very badly and expected to do
far more than was normal in a pastoral placement. I raised these
concerns with the Dean of Students who also looked after pas-

toral placements but all I got from him was that life can be a challenge sometimes and perhaps things would get better. They didn't and I hated the placement which sticks out in my mind as the most pointless placement I had in my seven years of pastoral work whilst in Clonliffe. Was it a test to see how I would get on or was it just too much bother for the Dean to find another placement that late in the year? Who knows, but I did gain an insight into what the future held in store when I got talking to one of the staff at the office.

She worked with a certain aspect of the programme provided by the organisation, as did her partner, and she always seemed very interested in my training and how I was getting on. I just valued the fact that somebody was being nice to me, but one day she was very upset and then the news broke that her partner was being let go from the staff. I asked her what was going on and she told me that he had been a priest in another diocese and had left, and that 'someone' in authority had taken exception to him working in a church organisation whilst living with his girlfriend. I was shocked at the apparent pettiness of what had happened. but their experience came back into my mind many times over the next number of years. What had they done that was so wrong as to merit such harsh treatment? I never did find out how things went for them as I lost touch with them as the pastoral placements ended at Easter.

My 21st birthday party was a big celebration in more ways than one, because I was delighted to leave such an unhappy working environment. I had to have my party during the Easter holidays as the college authorities frowned on events like these taking place during term time, for some reason which was never fully explained to any of us.

Towards the end of Third Year the time for our Pastoral Year placements to be announced drew closer. Holy Cross College ran an extra year for many of the students that saw the student work (unpaid of course) in an area of expertise that would stand him in good stead in the future. I had been asked what I would like to do for the year. I really wanted to go to the army for the year, as had happened to other students in the past, but deep down I knew that I would never be sent, given my interest in all things military. I wasn't sure what else I wanted to do so I thought that prison chaplaincy might be a good idea and opted for this. As happens so many times in the church, one should never ask for what one really wants to do, because experience shows one may never get it. Instead of being sent as an assistant prison chaplain I was assigned to a hostel for homeless boys, many of whom had been abused. This placement was for the first half of the year and then I was to train as an addiction counsellor at an alcohol and substance abuse unit on Dublin's north side. To say I was unimpressed was an understatement and I said so when asked. However, given my experience in the year just past, I knew the futility of asking for the year to be changed and resigned myself to what lay ahead.

Another of our classmates now left to join the year ahead as he had worked before entering the seminary and it was deemed unnecessary for him to do the pastoral year. The pastoral year worked in a similar way the Transition Year works in secondary schools – it ensures that students are at the correct age when leaving. This was also to fulfil the requirements of Canon Law that required a man to be 24 years of age in order to be ordained deacon and 25 in order to be ordained priest. This was part of the reason why seminarians who entered straight after school had to undertake the fourth year in Dublin.

As the summer loomed and the priesthood invitations started to come out, many of us were being asked to sing or serve at the ordinations. I was asked to cantor at a number of the ordinations and was also asked to be M2 (second master of ceremonies) at the ordination of a deacon I knew well. Then one morning the news broke that a number of the deacons were not being ordained. Nobody knew what was going on, only that the

Archbishop had intervened and, despite the protests of the President, the deacons were not to be ordained. A cloud was cast over the end of the year and we all went on holidays wondering what had happened.

I spent the summer learning to be a commuter, as I was working in a shop in Dublin and continuing to train with the Civil Defence for our annual training camp. I discovered in the weeks coming up to the camp that I had been promoted to Third Officer and was in charge of all communications for the exercise on the camp. I was absolutely delighted and, not for the first time, asked myself did I really want to continue training as a priest when so many other options were out there for me, if I really tried. The exercise went well and soon the time to return to college loomed once more.

My fourth year in seminary already. I really was unhappy with what lay ahead and had some curious looks from the Dean because I wasn't saying anything to him about it. Those who know me can read me like a book and I was clearly very unhappy. I knew there was no point in fighting with the authorities about the placement so I didn't waste my energy – maybe I was copping on to playing the system at last.

The crazy thing about my new post was that I had undertaken no interview to see if I had any aptitude for the job, never met any staff and didn't even know where the place was. Such was the preparation that went into the pastoral placements of Holy Cross College: 'This is where you are going; this is what you are going to do – off you go!' I managed to find the hostel after about an hour of searching and met some of the staff who were just going off shift. I was then sent off to the local doctor's surgery with one of the residents to 'have him checked for an STD'. I didn't know what an STD was and calmly announced to the receptionist that the boy was here to be checked for an STD. She looked startled and told us to wait. Then we went in and I repeated the same to the doctor, who remarked at how blasé I was about the fact. I then told him it was my first day and didn't know what an STD was. This doctor was very kind and informed me that the boy did not have a *sexually transmitted disease* after all. I was shocked and asked the staff member later on was that a wind up and she told me that it wasn't. The boy was in the care of the home due to the fact that he was being abused by a member of his family. This was my first introduction to the whole world of child abuse – little did I know how widespread a problem in our society it really was, and still is.

I worked in the hostel as a full member of staff, the only difference being was I worked for free – I got a travelling allowance from the college but was asked to return the change if there was any left over! How many people today would to a 24 hour shift and then hand over the change from their travelling allowance?

I encountered many sad stories of serial abuse and neglect, met alleged abusers and many victims who were too afraid to speak out. This was also the one and only time I knowingly came in contact with people working in the sex industry. Some of the residents had worked as rent boys when on the streets as it was the only way to get money to eat. I remember asking one of the lads if he was gay, as in my innocence I thought a person had to be gay to be a rent boy: 'I am not gay,' he said 'but I tell you what I am on the streets, cold, wet and hungry. If someone offers you a takeaway and £20 for a blowjob, it is hard to say no. There is a lot a person can do when they are hungry and desperate.' This really threw me back on my heels. I have never known lasting hunger or real poverty, and to hear someone be so upfront about the harsh realities of life on the street really made me think. The food in college didn't seem so bad afterwards either.

Given that a number of the boys had been in the sex industry, I wondered at the logic of placing the hostel in the middle of the red light district on Dublin's south side. Every night the 'ladies of the night' would ply the trade in all weathers. From Thursday to Sunday night the volume of traffic would increase and the vast majority of the cars were from the higher end of the market. We could observe the goings on from the upper windows (boys were fined if they were caught, but the staff often looked out). I remember one night seeing a pimp waiting behind a tree to take his 'cut' off the girl as soon as she got out of a car, and on another occasion seeing a prostitute get out of one car and into another in the space of two minutes. Business was brisk in spite of the new killer disease AIDS doing the rounds at the time. I remember a very funny but at the same time sad event one night. It was the practice for the Pastoral Year students to come together on a Friday night for tea and then a class get together with the Dean. It was also normal for us all to go for a pint afterwards but one Friday night in four I had to work, so on a wet November Friday night with the words of two classmates ringing in my ears – 'we are already doing what you are all striving to do' – I set off across the city to work. 'Already doing what you are striving for, my arse' I thought to myself as I trudged along in the rain. These two members of my year had been placed in parishes for their pastoral assignment and were 'shadowing' priests in the parish, experiencing what it was like to work as a priest, hence the jibe about already doing what the rest of us were striving to do. Their attitude and the fact that they were going off for pints and then a takeaway and I was on the 'graveyard shift' in the hostel did little to improve my mood. I was about 10 minutes from the hostel when I made the fatal mistake of saying goodnight to a person standing under a streetlight. I had been so preoccupied feeling sorry for myself that I hadn't noticed who I had said goodnight to. One of *cailíní na hoíche*, as the staff had begun re-ferring to the ladies of the night *as gaeilge*! 'Cold night, love, isn't it?' says the lady of the night. 'Yes' I reply, moving on. 'Not doing anything tonight love?' she replies. God, what do I say now? 'Ehm, no, I don't think I could afford it, sorry.' Then the saddest thing I had heard in ages – 'How much have you got?' Things were obviously slow and she was so desperate for money that she was willing to haggle for the price of her favours! I ran to the hostel and recounted the story to my colleagues who had a great laugh at the poor woman trying to wring a knock down session out of the seminarian. I think she would have found it funny too. I might even have got a clergy discount!

At the end of my time in the hostel I was sad to leave it, as I had come to enjoy working there and I also enjoyed cooking for the boys at the weekend. They didn't like my bacon and cabbage – all the staff did though, funnily enough – but my Saturday night fry-ups became very popular with all, especially the fried bread. The staff took a dim view of the food but the religious sister in charge approved it as a treat if all was well in the house. I have learnt now as a parent that it is better for children to eat something they like, within reason, rather than force them to eat something they don't want.

After Christmas it was off to the rehab centre and to learn to be a counsellor. This was a completely different set up as I worked more normal hours but had to do a lot of group work and sit-ins on one-to-one sessions until the time came for me to take clients on my own. This was a daunting task but I came to really enjoy doing this, far more than working in the hostel as it turned out. Maybe the Dean knew more about me and my potential than I thought. My time in the rehab centre made me realise that alcohol and drug abuse respects no social boundaries or career paths. One can become dependent on alcohol, drugs, cigarettes or sex regardless of whom or what one is or where one comes from. The Alcoholics Anonymous twelve steps programme really helps people to regain the dignity and self respect they have lost through drink, once they have accepted being powerless over alcohol. One aspect of my experience in the rehabilitation world is that when I am stressed or upset about something I go off alcohol completely. I don't know why but it is just an ingrained response to pressure in my own life.

Maybe it is in light of what I saw, but the bottle is an ever present spectre in the life of clergy of all denominations and regardless of marital status, and many clergy are part of recovery programmes whilst many others continue to console themselves with alcohol, destroying their health and ministry in many cases.

It was our turn to be invited into Senior Theology and this was a tense time, because one of us would be off to Rome and another off to Maynooth. However, things were different this year as a new President had been appointed to the college at the start of our Pastoral Year but we had had little contact with him. It was the tradition for us to be called up to the President in order of seniority to find out if we were going into Fifth Year but also where we were going. A new brush sweeps clean, as they say, and our senior man went up first and found he was off to Rome but also that the rest of us were staying in Dublin. This was the first time the link with Maynooth had been broken. The decline in numbers was beginning to show even in 1990. The decision was made to maintain the Dublin presence in Rome but not to send anyone to Maynooth. As it turned out, everybody ended up in Maynooth in the new millennium.

It was now June 1990 and I had arranged to work in the record company of a cousin in England. I stayed with my cousin and his family and had a great time working as the despatch clerk in his record company. I really enjoyed my time in London and was back on track for the move into Senior Theology.

It was now my turn to go into Senior House and start learning what it was to work as a priest. Many of my doubts now seemed silly as I was full of the notion that I was now in 'Senior House' and ordination was now really in sight. However, on the first night back I learned that two more classmates had not returned with us to Fifth Year, one by choice and one had been dismissed. Out of the fourteen who entered in 1986, we now numbered six in Dublin and one in Rome. By the beginning of Fifth year we had lost exactly 50% of our class. As was the custom, we gained two new classmates – one stayed back a year to complete his Masters in Arts and another moved up a year, skipping the Pastoral Year. So we were now eight in total – how many would see Ordination Day? Still the obsession with being ordained and never a thought as to what lay beyond …

CHAPTER THREE

Senior House days

We were back living in Senior House, facing Minor Orders (the first ministries on the way to ordination) and also about to become assistant chaplains in the various prisons in the city. I was also landed with the detested job of Refectorian. My daily task was to ensure that everybody had signed in/out for meals, that the numbers tallied and that those on wash-up did the job as it should have been done. An added complication was the fact that the 'Top Table' had been done away with by the new President the year before. The top table was where the priests had always eaten their lunch in the Refectory – all their other meals were in the Priests" Parlour – their private dining room. The venerable gentlemen were not the best at signing in and out for meals and I had a constant struggle to make numbers add up. This was the first time I was referred to as a good Sergeant Major.

Theology classes were interesting because this was the first time in four years of training that we were finally learning about the business of priesthood. Towards the end of the term we received the first order on the road to priesthood, that of Lector. We were now empowered to read in church. It didn't mean much as we had been reading in church since we entered college, but for those of us desperate to move on it was a step in the right direction.

This desire to get through the system and be ordained seems odd now but was, as I have already said earlier, a normal part of seminary life when I was there. Is this an indication of 'brainwashing' or simply a case of an immature man caught up in the whole notion of priesthood and ordination? I still try to answer this question about my time in seminary. It would be easy to say that I was simply brain-washed and all of what happened earlier was not my fault, but the environment in which I was living was a very tightly controlled way of life: first bell a 6.45 am, second bell at 7.25 am; church service at 7.30 am; breakfast at 8.15 am; lectures from 9am to 10.35 am; coffee until 11 am; lectures from 11 am until 12.30 pm; lunch at 1 pm; free time/study until 5.45 pm; church service until 6.30 pm: tea from 6.30 pm until 7/7.15 pm; pastoral work/study/spiritual direction/recreation until 10 pm; optional night prayer until 10.15 pm; retire by 11.30 pm. This was the normal routine of a day in Clonliffe during my time there. I recall vividly looking out the window of the main corridor one day and realising that I had not set foot outside of the college building in over a week. I was studying for my Sixth Year winter exams and had been excused pastoral work as I was unwell, but not to have stepped outside in a week! This was a sign of how cosseted I had become within the system and I was not the only one. A system that can encourage a man to live in such a reclusive manner must be reviewed, but I accepted this as a normal part of my life. I rarely wondered about what my life would be like later on, other than to wonder what kind of house I would live in and what kind of car I would drive. Yes, I really was this shallow at this time in my life.

My pastoral placement in Fifth Year was the long term prison on Dublin's north side and so I went every Wednesday and Sunday and mingled with many convicted of murder, manslaughter, child abuse and serious sexual crimes. As it tuned out I knew a good number of the prison officers as we were all from the same Civil Defence units, and as soon as the prisoners discovered this I was ostracised by them and referred to as 'Fr Screw', screw being the term used by prisoners when referring to prison officers. I wasn't upset as I felt that the prison staff was often neglected by some of the pastoral team who spent a lot of their energies on the prisoners. I spent my time in the prison chatting to the officers and those prisoners who would talk to me. I enjoyed the placement immensely and regretted not spending my pastoral year as a prison chaplain.

In December of 1990 my grandfather died after suffering a massive stroke and a huge influence in my life was gone forever. I had worked with him in my summer jobs, learned to drive pony and traps with him and firmly believe that my ability to speak with no notes and preach at the drop of a hat comes from Pop, who was a wonderful story teller and song writer. He had always enjoyed going to mass in Clonliffe on a Sunday and delighted in the respect shown him by my fellow students. I was saddened that no one from the college staff had attended the funeral and I heard later that a member of staff had said it was only a grand parent and as such didn't merit staff members going to the funeral.

After Christmas the next step on the road to priesthood came along and we were conferred with the Order of Acolyte, meaning that we were now ministers of the Eucharist. The next step would be Candidacy for Ordination the following year. We worked hard in class and had to complete a large numbers of essays and projects in preparation for the following year's studies. We were also getting used to the new Dean of Students who was far different to the previous man and was quite unpopular amongst many of the students. I spent the summer working at home and reading theology – it amazes me now just how into the whole thing I really was at this stage in my training. The doubts were there all the time but I just put them down to being nervous. I don't think I really allowed myself to consider the prospect of not being ordained as at this time it was an unthinkable prospect, or so I thought. I was so enthusiastic about ministry that I actually requested to begin my new pastoral placement early. As one friend has commented since, it was like I had become a different person, totally switched into priesthood and nothing else. When I look back at this time I can in some respects identify with members of a religious cult who are totally wrapped up in what they believe and refuse to accept any criticism of what they are part of. Ordination was my goal and I was giving it all I had. Again I have to ask myself the question –was I brainwashed? Perhaps for a time I was, but the reality of serving as a priest would soon remove any conditioning away forever.

I was appointed to a parish on the north side of Dublin, on what has often been referred to as the 'Gold Coast' by clergy – a line of parishes from Howth in the north to Killiney in the south. I don't think anyone needs me to explain why they are referred to as golden parishes. I would remain in this parish until I was ordained priest and was to learn the day to day skills of being a priest from the parish clergy. There was a parish priest, a curate and a parish chaplain. I taught in the primary school, took some classes in the secondary school and visited homes in the parish as well as having Sunday duties. I took to parish work like a duck to water, so the big question as to what area of priesthood was for me seemed to be answered. We were being repeatedly asked to consider teaching, chaplaincy or parish ministry as options after ordination. I also enjoyed the camaraderie amongst the clergy – that made what was to come all the harder to believe and accept.

So I now had a parish placement to help me start to learn the skills that I would use after ordination. Sixth Year in Clonliffe was a busy year as a lot of the marks to qualify for the Bachelor in Divinity degree in the final year of the theology course would result from the two sets of examinations in this year. Our homiletics classes also became more demanding as we were now preaching 'on camera', and also preaching to invited congregations who had score sheets to mark our sermons out of 10 for interest, content, length and so on. I remember making a point at one of these 'rent a crowd' sessions and using my hand to count 1, 2, 3 and so on. Afterwards one of the commentators expressed concerns that the student had given the congregation the two finger salute! Either I had my hand facing the wrong way or the commentator was short sighted, but it sticks in my mind still and I am most careful about hand signals from the pulpit ever since.

A warning of the storm that was to come arose in Canon Law class one morning. Our lecturer was talking to us about celibacy and the numbers of priests leaving the church who wanted to marry and have a family. We asked him about his own year and he reminded us that many of the priests of his era had gone through seminary at the time of the Second Vatican Council, a time of great hope and potential rebirth in the church. The mass would be celebrated in the language of the people and not Latin, many moves on ecumenical relations were promulgated and the question of priestly celibacy was being discussed. A lot of clergy and seminarians firmly believed that an optional promise of celibacy would be introduced in the Roman Catholic Church, similar to that in the Orthodox and Eastern churches, and some actually went ahead with ordination in spite of being unhappy but in the hope that celibacy would soon be an option, not an imposition. Our lecturer believed that many of those who had left since then had grown increasingly disillusioned as the reforms of the Second Vatican Council were bogged down and in some cases reversed. He exhorted us to look long and hard at our commitment to celibacy and if we felt we could not live that way of life then better to leave now rather than later.

He then dropped a bombshell into the conversation. He also asked us to think long and hard about our disposition towards relationships with men and children. I was shocked at this – I knew that a number of priests were gay and had been propositioned by a priest one afternoon in my Third Year, so the notion of gay clergy was not a new one to me. (I nearly died of shock that afternoon and tried to be as polite as possible without being offensive. God pardon my innocence.) However, the idea that someone would have a sexual relationship with a child was a sickening reality that I had encountered in my Pastoral Year, but the idea that a priest would do this! My reaction was that of countless people from a generation who believed that clergy were beyond reproach. Our lecturer intimated that a case was brewing in another diocese that would change the church forever and how right he was.

Shortly after returning to college in January 1992, we were asked by the President if we were prepared to go forward to be ordained as deacons. We had just had a huge water fight on our corridor – some things hadn't changed in six years – and down he arrived with a big smirk on his face, asking us if we wanted to become clerics. The first step was to write a letter to the Archbishop requesting that we be admitted as candidates for ordination to the diaconate. This letter had to be written on headed college stationary and written in our own hands so that our request could be verified as being made freely and without coercion. The standing joke was that we had to go home and consult with our vocations – our mothers! This may have been the case for some priests in the past but I can say in all honestly we all took this next step of our own free will. I say this and yet I still wonder how free I really was.

I had toyed with the idea of leaving the priesthood from time to time but cannot say that I gave it any serious contemplation other than to wonder what people would think of me if I left. My parents always supported me fully and had told me many times that they would support me if I decided to leave but I do believe that I was caught up completely in the desire to become an ordained priest. Perhaps I felt I wanted to prove to myself that I could do it, but I do not think that I really took fully into account the long term implications that priesthood would have for me. Again and again I found myself disagreeing with issues raised in lectures but put these disagreements to the back of my mind when the discussion of ordination was raised.

A very insightful priest passed the comment during my first

year that one could go along in college in a trance and wake up one morning about to be ordained a deacon, and he was right, it did seem to have happened all very quickly. We received the order of Candidate and we were now just months away from becoming clerics at long last.

During the spring of 1992, an unusual event occurred in the parish I was working in. The parish chaplain had good links with Medjugorje and invited Fr Slavko and two of the visionaries to come and speak at a youth mass. Medjugorje is located in Bosnia and it is believed by many, but not officially promulgated by the church, that the Blessed Virgin appeared to a number of young people, and allegedly continues to do so. Many Irish people have travelled there over the years and the word of the impending visit soon got around. On the Sunday afternoon of the mass, the parish was thronged with people and the biggest task for the parish team was to keep people back from mobbing the visionaries. I have never experienced religious mania/fervour before but some of the people attending the mass looked on the visionaries as if they were Jesus Christ himself and I was unnerved at the wide-eyed stare of a very small number of the faithful in the church. I remember after the mass being in the priest's house where we were entertaining our celebrity visitors, when I walked out of the kitchen straight into two people who had sneaked in through the unlocked back door. I had to ask them to leave but they wept when I said they couldn't see the visionaries. I was really perturbed at this reaction and wondered what need was being fed within people like this by searching out the visionaries in this manner.

The date for our ordination as deacons was set for Easter Sunday, 19 April 1992. We had been asked about what date we would like for the ordination and we chanced our collective arms by asking for Easter Sunday as it would mean a whole week off after the big event. To our surprise, the Archbishop agreed and so the invitations could be printed and the planning began. The location for our diaconate retreat was chosen and we would be going to the Benedictine Monastery at Glenstal in Limerick with the college Spiritual Director. The location was great but I don't think any of us were happy at who would lead the retreat, as the college Spiritual Director was not an ideal choice in the eyes of the student body. The staff knew this but seemed unwilling or possibly unable to do anything about it. Surely the role of Spiritual Director was one that should have been monitored carefully? Did the authorities not notice that 85% of the students had a director other than the college director? The First Years had no choice but we all had and chose other directors as some of us felt that the resident director had nothing to offer us. Maybe this was the arrogance of youth, but I took exception to his abrupt manner and lack of interaction with the college body. How could he help us in our spiritual journey if he never bothered getting to know us?

We were now seven in our year, with another classmate studying in Rome, and then the news was broken to us by one of our classmates that he had been called up to see the President and that his ordination was being deferred pending a decision by the board of the college. This had upset him so much that he had decided to leave the college and not go forward for ordination. We did not know at the time that he had been told that he would never be ordained, and it was only long after our diaconate that we finally found out what had really been said. Naturally we were all saddened to lose yet another classmate at this late stage and we really didn't know what was going on. Nothing changed insofar as the authorities didn't seem to care about the impact their actions would have on the rest of the class. The fact that someone we had lived with for a number of years was gone was never addressed or officially referred to by the authorities.

CHAPTER FOUR

Holy Orders approach

We went on retreat, glad to be getting away from lectures and the strained atmosphere in the college after the departure of our classmate. We took the train to Limerick and were picked up and brought out to the Abbey. Our rooms were basic but comfortable and we joined the community for worship and meals, whilst having sessions with the Spiritual Director in the morning and evening. I enjoyed the break and felt that I was prepared for what was ahead of us in the coming weeks.

We went back to the seminary to face the build up to ordination and got through the Easter ceremonies in a trance. (At least I did.) I must say that the Easter Vigil mass in my parish was very memorable as my deacon's stoles were blessed at the mass and I went back to college that night ready for the next day. Was I stressed? I think the fact that I had an ulcer under my right armpit the size of an old pound coin would be a good indication of how wound up and worn out I was at the time.

Easter Sunday 1992 dawned a lovely sunny day and we were all up early, preparing ourselves for the day's events. We attended morning prayer in the Oratory and the level of support I received from all those around us was quite unlike anything I had experienced in my previous six years in the college. We gathered in the Communications Room (a small oratory used to learn to say mass whilst being filmed) on the lower corridor shortly before the mass, to robe and then go in procession to the church. This was the first time we had all dressed in our own albs and clerical dress. We entered that church as six laymen, and would leave it as members of the clergy. Walking into the church, a place I had been in hundreds of times before, filled to capacity with family and friends, the thurible billowing out clouds of incense and the choir singing 'Praise the Lord all you nations' really took my breath away and I remember the ceremony as being very special. Vivid memories are the look on my parents' faces to the Archbishop embracing each one of us and saying 'Welcome brother'. I can't remember much of the party afterwards but it really was a magical day and I was very glad to have a week off to recover from it all.

So now, at long last, after six years and many ups and downs, I was a member of the clergy of the Roman Catholic Church. People were very polite and smiled saying 'Hello, Father' if they didn't know me and many friends now seemed unsure of how to be around me given my newly ordained status. About three weeks after I became a deacon, the news broke that a bishop of the Roman Catholic Church in Ireland had resigned amid rumours of financial and moral impropriety. It soon emerged that Bishop Eamonn Casey had resigned because a newspaper was about to go public with the story that he had fathered a child with an American woman. The attitude of people in the street changed overnight. Whereas people had been very polite one day, the next day many were openly scathing and mocking of anyone in a collar. It was almost as if the people now had a chance to vent their real feelings against injustices, real or perceived, that they may have felt were visited upon them by the clergy.

No sooner had the college geared back up for the last term than the examination timetables appeared. The results from my theology exams would be added up and, if I reached a certain standard, I would qualify for the Bachelor of Divinity degree course. What we didn't realise was that the course was about to change from a general and honours course to an honours course only. We were also waiting to hear what parishes we would be assigned to for the summer, as it was the tradition for the new deacons from the Archdiocese of Dublin to work in London for six weeks during the summer holidays. I asked the Dean of Students when we would be learning how to conduct baptisms, weddings and funerals, which are all part of the duties of a deacon. He smiled at me and told me I would pick it up as I went along! I was speechless – six years of studies and no preparation worth talking about for sacraments. If it wasn't for our homiletics lecturer, who independently undertook to train us in these areas shortly before the summer break began, we would have gone to our parishes with absolutely no sacramental preparation at all.

I was assigned to a parish in the east end of London. I made contact with my parish priest and arranged to meet at Stansted Airport after the summer ordinations were over. Before I set off for the summer we had two celebrations in my parish – the parish chaplain was nominated as president of the Canon Law Society of the British Isles and also celebrated his 25th anniversary of ordination. His full time job was working in the Marriage Tribunal in Archbishop's House. Imagine the impact when many couples found out that the priest deciding their future (in the area of marriage annulment) ended up being convicted and imprisoned for paedophile activity. This came as a huge shock to many of us, even though some still find that fact hard to accept. I have often been accused of knowing something but it was as much a shock to me as many of the parishioners. However, that knowledge was a year away to most of us and we celebrated these two milestones in his career with a big party and everyone was delighted for him.

I took part in a number of the ordination ceremonies as deacon and had even started planning my own ordination that would take place the following year. Patience is not one of my virtues, as anyone who knows me will tell you. The summer carried on and soon London was calling and I travelled to Stansted with a classmate and we headed off to our parishes in Essex. At first I was very unsure of the set up I was in. The Parish Priest seemed very formal and the curate was extremely rude and full of his own importance. However, I got to know the PP as time went on and came to value him as a dear friend. Sadly, little happened to change my opinion of the curate. In fact, if I really think about it, the Parish Priest was the type of priest I wanted to be, at that time. I thoroughly enjoyed my time in the parish, marvelling at the unity and spirit of the Roman Catholic Church in England. The only church I can compare it to in Ireland is the Church of Ireland. There was a great sense of living within one's own community and helping each other as much as one could. I did commit a mortal sin whilst on a visit to the diocesan cathedral when I sat on the bishop's throne. It appears that no one is allowed to sit on it apart from the bishop – ooops! Maybe that was when the rot started to set in between me and the Roman Catholic Church.

I took the opportunity to visit some of my family whilst I was in Britain but also spent my days off in the many military museums and militaria shops in London. It was on such a trip that I looked into an army recruiting office again and the recruiting sergeant caught my eye and beckoned me in. He asked if I was interested in joining up? As I was in plain clothes he had no idea that I was a cleric. I asked him about recruitment possibilities for chaplains and he gave me a lot of information and said the army was always looking for chaplains. There it was again – the pull towards the military way of life whilst at the same time wanting to be a priest. I went off with confusion starting to rear its ugly little head again. What did I really want to do in the future and was it a silly question now that I was already a cleric?

When we returned to college in September 1992 it was hard to believe that this would be the last time I would return to college for another year. We were now the senior year and I have to confess that I was a very angry, self absorbed individual who was very unpleasant to a lot of the people around me. I was stressed, anxious and in a hurry to be ordained and get out of Clonliffe. I decided not to bother having much to do with the communal life of the college. As a result I didn't make much effort to get to know the new students or get involved in the recreational events in the course of the year. I was grumpy, waspish and terribly taken with being a cleric. These were all symptoms of a person who was very unhappy and unsure, but I was too absorbed to see this at the time.

I was now facing the reality of being a cleric and for the first time I started asking myself had I made the right decision? I assisted at a number of marriages where friends from home were getting married. I could see the joy they had at the prospect of their lives together and I was also baptising babies and saw the joy on the faces of the new parents. I was facing the prospect of growing into old age as a single man and, if I am honest, I am not sure that the prospect filled me with any great joy. Was I cut out to be a celibate for the rest of my life? Celibacy hadn't posed that much of a challenge thus far, apart from one or two fleeting relationships with women whilst a junior student. It now finally dawned on me that the promise I was to make at priesthood would be final and I needed to think about it. A little late, you might say, but it was a subject that was rarely, if ever, spoken about either officially or amongst ourselves. Celibacy within the ministerial priesthood is a great gift and is liberating for those that are truly called to the vocation of celibacy, and many within the Roman Catholic and Reformed churches are called to and live a fulfilled celibate life. There are also many called to the priesthood in both the Roman Catholic and Reformed churches but who are not called to a celibate way of life and many clergy in the Reformed churches live a much fulfilled life as married clerics. I do not intend to preach to anybody, but an optional vow of celibacy has served the Orthodox churches well for many centuries and proves that a deacon-elect deciding whether or not to live as a celibate priest or as a married person can and does work. It is not for me to preach to my birth church but many people of all traditions would welcome a full and open debate on this issue.

At the beginning of my final year, I was informed that I had been selected to complete an honours Bachelor of Divinity. I had wanted to write my degree thesis on the question of priestly celibacy from the middle of sixth year, and in anticipation of getting the correct amount of marks to do the degree I had completed a good amount of research over the summer holidays. How foolish I was to think that anything had changed for me in the college as I learned early in September 1992 that I was not going to be allowed to complete a thesis on my chosen topic. The reason I was given for this decision was, admittedly in my own opinion, unsatisfactory: 'We feel it is not a good idea to write a thesis about the way of life you will be living.' I wondered what kind of a church I was joining if it couldn't even ask itself searching questions, albeit through the medium of a seminarian's degree thesis? Eventually I picked a subject that I was allowed to write a thesis on – the care of the dying and the response from medical ethics. I did enjoy the research needed to write the thesis and my moderator was hard but fair. The research into this area of medical care has stood me in good stead in my ministry, but I still wonder at what harm a thesis on the subject of priestly celibacy could have done.

The final year in Clonliffe was so busy it was hard to think about what lay ahead the following summer. We had a full schedule of lectures, extra classes required to bring us up to speed in sacramental duties, a thesis to prepare whilst also working in our parishes and taking a full part in the liturgical life of the college and the nearby enclosed convent.

I had really started to wonder what the future held for me in terms of how my life as a priest would be. Routine in the college had almost an anaesthetic affect and you could float along, keeping the future firmly at the back of your mind. It seemed to me that all my classmates wanted to talk about was the type of vestments they would wear, how big a chalice they needed and the importance of wearing black clerical dress at all times.

I was sitting in the coffee room one night with two of my classmates and I raised the subject of marriage and children. To be honest, I was sick of the endless round of talk about ordination and decided to stir things up a bit. I asked them if they really were happy with the prospect of never having a partner and children. I had known these men since I was 18 and thought I really knew them well, but when they told me that there was no way they ever wanted a family I was really thrown. They asked me how I felt about it and when I said I would like a family but was unsure about it all, they tore a strip off me and told me to pull myself together or else I would be in trouble later on. How right they were, but in a way in which neither they nor I could possibly have imagined at that time.

It was around October 1992 that I was called to see the Dean of Students to 'chat' about things. I disliked him and knew that his little chats rarely meant good news. He had decided that I 'needed' to go for counselling which would help prepare me for ordination. I told him that I felt that this was unnecessary but he then implied that if I refused to go for counselling, my suitability for ordination would have to be reviewed. From my own training as a counsellor, albeit brief, I knew that the first rule is that a person must go to counselling of their own free will to benefit from the experience. As I was going under duress, whatever benefits I may have derived from counselling were already in doubt. It seemed that my whole year was being made attend different counsellors, much to our disgust.

The first lady I went to broke many of the basic rules of good practice: she sat with her back to a window so that I could not see her face; she did most of the talking and used whatever I said to throw back at me in a very confrontational manner. I eventually got up and left and told her I would not be coming back.

I told the Dean of my experience and he was annoyed but arranged for me to see someone else way over on the south side of the city. I was expected to find and fund my own way there, even though I was still without any income. This counsellor was a very strange individual, very interested in my sex life (that conversation was over quickly as there was little to talk about) and my development as a child. Many sessions were spent painting pictures whilst she kept on at me about whether I was worried about life or not. I really didn't gain much from the sessions and almost laughed at her when she wondered if the fact that my ordination would be at the end of all the others was a sign that the diocese had 'it in for me'. I assured her that the date suited the bishop, my parish and I best, but she seemed to think that there was another agency at work behind the scenes. All I can say about my experiences of diocesan-funded counselling is that if I wasn't paranoid beforehand, there was a good likelihood of it afterwards.

As the year rolled on, we began to have more and more night classes in preparation for ministry. A number of the sessions on the sacrament of confession were very interesting and we even had 'mock' penitents to try out our skills on, with prepared sins of course. The object of this exercise was to see how well we could think on our feet in a difficult pastoral situation. It brought home to me just how good some of our lectures could have been, had they been more practically based, rather than relying solely on books. It was around this time that we were also given a tour of the long term care facility in one of the Dublin hospitals that caters for people in comas. This was of great interest to me, given the subject of my thesis, but it also brought home to me that there are many types of vocation, not just religious ones.

Ordination was drawing closer and as time went on booklets had to be drawn up, invitations printed and sent, and vestments made or bought. I viewed the whole process of getting vestments with dread as I had gone through the various catalogues which seemed to be multiplying on our corridor by the day. I just wanted a plain white chasuble (the priest's outer vestment worn during mass) but this seemed a very tall order for many of the vestment suppliers, so a cousin volunteered to make one for me. I also had qualms about spending so much money on a silver chalice and paten (cup and plate). What I really wanted was a pottery chalice. Did I have an option for the poor? No, I just found the whole cost attached to ordination distasteful. We were being ordained to serve the community and could I justify spending thousands when there was no need to? On the practical side, my parents bought my first car for me for the same amount of money that some of my classmates spent on their chalices.

The final examinations were drawing closer and it was a much pressurised time for all of us. We had to take exams in scripture, moral theology, church history, canon law, systematic theology, and Hebrew. The main subjects had written and oral parts and many hours were spent revising lecture notes from 1986-87 (First Theology) and 1990-1993 (Second, Third and Fourth Theology). I made a mess of my moral theology oral exam – I think it was tiredness as I had done all the revision – but I managed to redeem myself in the written paper. The nastiest little exam of all was the faculties exam. This was to see if we knew enough about what we had learned in theology and canon law to practice as priests. It was held on the morning of the Deacon's Farewell Dinner, traditionally the day when everybody moved up a year. I went into my faculties exam totally exhausted and just kept repeating that 'the seal of confession is inviolable' despite being thrown all kinds of questions by the two examiners. I passed this final hurdle and went upstairs to continue packing, as we were heading off to Mellifont Cistercian Abbey for our priesthood retreat that evening.

CHAPTER FIVE

Priesthood beckons

We were finished – seven years of lectures, pastoral work, challenges from the staff, awful food, boarding school bullying, and many sad and funny moments! All was now finished and the next stage was retreat and ordination. Had it really been seven years? It only seemed like yesterday that this naïve 18-year-old walked in through the college door, and now a cynical and not necessarily wiser but definitely greyer 25-year-old was walking back out to face an uncertain future.

The farewell dinner was good fun, the usual teasing being made at the expense of the outgoing class. I was, according to the speaker, being appointed to the Glencree Centre for Peace and Reconciliation – a very pointed but also very accurate comment given the angry and unfriendly person I had become in the last few years at the college.

We left and made our individual ways to the Abbey in County Louth. I checked in and lay down on my bed and woke three hours later to find the Guest Master shaking my foot, fearful that I was unwell as he had found it so hard to wake me from the exhausted sleep I had fallen into.

The retreat was wonderful. We had picked our own director and he really did us proud – it was the best retreat I had ever been on and none has compared to it since either. The director had been one of our lecturers when we were junior students and he had left a deep impression on us all.

I returned home to Newcastle after the retreat, to prepare for my own ordination whilst attending the ordinations of my classmates. It was scary to see them going through what I was also facing but the support of family and friends really helped at this time. As all of this was going on, the priests I had worked with in my placement parish were also involved in my ordination. The curate was my Master of Ceremonies and the parish chaplain would robe me as a priest. I thought he was very preoccupied at the time of my ordination. It was only afterwards that I learned that he was in the process of making a legal settlement with one of his victims. However, he took a full part in my ordination and carried on as if all was fine in the world. I would ponder this fact many times once the story had been brought out into the public arena.

The church in which I was to be ordained celebrated its 25th anniversary the week before my ordination (the real reason for my ordination being late, not some Machiavellian plot by the diocese) and it really set the scene for my ordination. The village of Kilcoole was prepared, the church redecorated and the grounds landscaped, all in anticipation of the coming events. A whole week of 25th celebrations took place and it meant that I was very busy coming up to 20 June, the day on which I would be ordained a priest to serve God and the community to which I would be appointed following my ordination.

I spent the night before my ordination with friends who had been a good support to me in my placement parish and who also bought my chalice and paten for me. The generosity of people at this time was staggering. A mass kit –the portable communion set used by all clergy – was left into a friend's house as an anonymous gift. In spite of the fact that I had my chalice and paten, another set was bought for me by well-wishers and many people gave me many gifts of money and religious items long before my ordination ever took place.

To say that I was nervous would be an understatement. I can only just remember the night of the rehearsal and hoped that everybody else would remember what they were doing, as I certainly wouldn't. The few days leading up to the ordination were very wet and we were all praying that the rain would lift. The great day dawned and it was lashing rain, but as the time for the ordination grew closer the weather cleared and by 2 pm the sun was struggling out of the clouds. I went to the church on my own and began to get ready. The traditional dress for ordination is alb and deacon's stole, worn over clerical dress, but being very traditional, I opted to wear my soutane under my alb – a choice I would later regret given the intense heat and humidity in the church that day.

The many priests who had been invited began to arrive and robe in the papal vestments, made for the Pope's visit in 1979 and used for all major diocesan events since. The procession formed up and we all moved towards the church for the ceremony to begin. I was amazed at the number of people who were filling up the church. I was the first ordination for the diocese in the church and a nice touch was the fact that the first priest ordained in the church – for a religious order – was home on leave and attended the ordination. The other two clerical sons of the parish were also there – the late Mgr Bob Gara, home from the USA on leave, and another deacon from the college, who would be ordained in the neighbouring church the following year.

The music was provided by the Diocesan Resource Group, based in Dublin and with whom I had sung many times when the college choir and group came together for large events. I processed in at the top of the procession and sat beside my parents, to symbolise a man called from among the people to serve the people. Looking back on the photographs now I looked tense, very warm and excited all at the same time and much of the ordination is a blur. I remember the sermon from the bishop, the lying on the ground for the litany and my hands being anointed with the holy oils. One vivid memory is the laying of hands by the bishop and all the priests present – many whispered words of encouragement were passed on at this time – and finally being robed for the first time as a priest. Little did I know at that point that one of the priests who robed me would serve a prison sentence for child abuse and the other priest would report me to the bishop a few years later for being involved with a woman who worked with me in one of my chaplaincies. I assumed my place alongside the main celebrants of the mass and administered Holy Communion to many family and friends.

The really hard part was yet to come for me. It is the tradition in the Roman Catholic Church that a newly ordained priest gives his 'first blessing' to all those at the ordination. The ordination ended by about 3.30 pm and for the next hour at least I imparted my blessings to all in the church. I have the funny feeling that a few came up more than once but I blessed so many people that day that it is still a complete blur to me. This really was a humbling experience, blessing people I had known all my life, as well as many strangers, but the emotion of this experience is evident from the photographs that were taken. I was very relieved to finally go across the road to the boys school (the successor to the school I had attended as a child) where the traditional 'bun fight' took place. I was overwhelmed at the number of people who were still at the school well over an hour after the mass had ended and it was great to see many friends, including some of my classmates who had left Clonliffe over the course of the years. A long night of partying ensued and then it was time for me to get my head around the prospect of saying mass on my own for the first time the next day.

Some people seem amazed when I describe the type of social events at ordination time. They say it sounds just like a wedding and in a way it is. The man to be ordained is 'married' to God and the church and everybody celebrates the event in time honoured fashion. My classmates were by and large having their ordination receptions at hotels but I decided to hold my reception in the local community centre as there was such a big crowd invited and many others expected to turn up on the day. Lots of friends of the family rowed in and worked hard to arrange everything for the meal and dance afterwards. The community centre was transformed and the tables all set and ready for the congregation who would come back after the 'First Mass'. No matter how many times I had attended mass in the past, this time I would be leading the celebration, I would be saying mass.

A different group was providing the music for my mass and I continued to break with tradition by refusing to preach at the mass. I was too stressed at the prospect of saying the mass properly and opted to ask someone to preach for me. I turned once again to my school chaplain and he agreed to preach for me. This was a great relief but I did get a lot of flak about it from my classmates who were horrified that I was breaking with tradition. I arrived at the church about an hour before the mass was due to begin and spent the time checking and rechecking that everything was ready. It is a practice I still observe to this day – arriving well before a service is due to begin to avoid being late and also to make sure that I am completely prepared for the service.

The time for the mass to begin came and I remember the huge number of people there, the heat and the reassurance that everybody was on my side. Another memory is very clear, the mother of my oldest friend from home, who had been battling cancer, made a huge effort to come to the church and seeing her there gave me great strength to get through the day. After the mass was over, those who had not received a blessing the day before queued up for me to bless them – quite a number seemed to be familiar from the day before but I guess the novelty of a first blessing had yet to wear off for many at the two day event! The reception was a great affair – plenty of food for all, the staff from a friend's restaurant served the meal and my cousin's band provided the music. I don't remember eating much and people's faces were a blur as everybody wanted to wish me well. From the photographs, everybody seemed to enjoy the day greatly and people still remind me about it on occasion. It is a testimony to the hard work and devotion of my parents that such a great event was planned and executed with very few upsets or disasters. It sounds like I was in a trance for both days but there was so much going on and so many people around me that much of the detail is hard to recall.

For the next week or so I was in a whirl of saying masses in peoples houses, at my primary school and attending other functions, one of which still makes me smile wryly to myself. In my fifth year in college I preached in a south side parish on Clonliffe Sunday, the day each year when the people of the Archdiocese got to see a seminarian and the seminarian then preached, or in reality begged for money for the college. On this particular Sunday I was entertained to lunch by the parish priest who was very friendly and he introduced me to another priest who helped out in the parish. This priest was a member of a religious society under the patronage of the late Pope John Paul II. The priest from this society was very friendly and I had heard of him through some of my classmates, many of whom he seemed to know well. I met him again from time to time and he attended both my diaconate and priesthood ordinations, much to the horror of some of the clergy of the diocese. My class were considered the most conservative ordained in years and that would have been a fair comment at the time. I too was very set in my ways and wary of change. I put this down to seven years living like a monk and a complete lack of experience about life in the real world. That would come soon enough!

Towards the end of June each year, the society holds a mass to mark the anniversary of the death of their founder. As it turned out, nearly all of my class were at this mass, quite a coup for the society to have so many of the newly ordained priests of the diocese in attendance. My parents were also invited and it was only through talking to a colleague later in the summer that I saw the other side of things. This society has another branch for diocesan clergy who takes vows to the society and upon their death, all the property of that priest reverts to the society. I heard of one priest whose mother lived with him and when he died unexpectedly, his mother was left with nothing belonging to her son, not even his prayer book as 'all belonged to the society'. At this point I began to gently distance myself and prepared for parish life. I went back to my parish in London for a week's holiday and was delighted to see so many friends once again – it would become a place of refuge for me when times were bad.

CHAPTER SIX

The Curate's Egg

About a week before I went on holiday I got my letter of appointment from the Archbishop, along with my *pajellum* – my licence to work as a priest. It turned out that I was being appointed curate in the parish next door to the parish where I had worked as a deacon. I was delighted at the prospect, especially as the other curate had been a priest in my home parish and the parish priest had been a member of the staff in Clonliffe so at least I knew who I would be working with.

I went out one afternoon to see the house I would be living in and to see how much had to be done to it but it wasn't too bad and Dad and I sorted out what needed doing. The parish priest also gave me some money to get started with and so began the process of setting up home for the first time. I never realised just how much goes into a house and that everything has to be bought – this shows how institutionalised I really was. I had about three weeks to get everything ready before I commenced my duties in the parish and it was very nice to be anonymous at that time. I was doing the garden one afternoon and a lady asked me would I do hers after I had finished doing up the garden for the new priest. I readily agreed and turned up at her door with a shovel, wearing my collar – the poor lady nearly dropped with fright, but little things like that broke the ice and let people know that I was a normal person.

One event really threw me and still sits uneasily on my shoulders to this day and reflects the mentality of many people towards priests at that time. I was returning to the parish after lunch with my former parish priest in the neighbouring parish.

As I was bringing him out as a thank you for all his kindness I wore formal clerical dress and was walking back to my car. An elderly man stopped me and asked me if I was the new priest in the parish. I said I was and he dropped to his knees to receive my blessing. This was bizarre enough, but then he took both my hands and kissed the palms where I had been anointed by the bishop. This really freaked me out, as the man seemed to think that I was so much better than him when clearly I was not.

The next two weeks were spent getting my first home up and running – changing names on bills, finding out how everything worked and learning to fend for myself – remember I had been looked after all the way through my seminary life so now it was reality time. I had just about got over the shock of fending for myself when it was time for me to be introduced to the parish. People had been popping in to say hello but this Saturday night was my first mass as curate of the parish. It came and went with a very warm welcome from everybody and I soon settled into the routine of daily mass, communion calls, school duties, hospital visits and all that goes with the role of a priest. I also had to face the reality of death as I was soon conducting the funerals of parishioners in my 'area' of responsibility. I got on well with the clergy – as I said earlier I had known both of them before and this made for a good working relationship, but this is not always the case.

The highpoints of my first year as a priest were celebrating Christmas mass and being involved in the Easter ceremonies fully. The volume of confessions surprised me and I felt sorry for some people clearly hung up on past sins and unable to let them go. The low points were dealing with tragic deaths. The one that comes immediately to mind was a death in a neighbouring parish (it was my day on call) of an elderly man who was dying at home. I was with him until he died and, as I was going, his wife thanked me for being with them as it was their 50th wedding anniversary that day ...

The following summer it was my turn to lead the parish pilgrimage to Lourdes and, whilst I enjoyed the whole experience, I came to realise that if I didn't do something about my weight I would suffer from poor health. I had really let myself go – it is easy to be very kind to yourself when you are the cook so I decided to start taking regular exercise. It soon became a familiar sight to see Fr Mark power walking up and down the coast road and pretty soon I noticed that I was losing weight. I was also appointed chaplain to a large secondary school in the area. This was in addition to my other duties and I received absolutely no training for the task, nor did I receive any remuneration for the role either.

My fellow curate in the parish was appointed to a new parish and his replacement would not come to the parish until after the summer. As the parish priest had arranged his holidays before the June moves, I opted to cover the parish for the duration of his holidays. It was an intensely busy time. I had to deal with a number of tragedies in the parish during this time and I began to realise just how lonely a life the ordained ministry can be if you let it get like that.

CHAPTER SEVEN

Questions and doubts begin

Life for the first two years of my appointment had fallen into a routine of visiting, sacramental duties and developing a keen interest in military history. However, a storm was brewing within our deanery (a geographical grouping of parishes within a diocese) that those on the ground had no inkling of. At this time, I started thinking about military chaplaincy again as a possible career path. I enquired with my bishop if there were any vacancies in the Irish Defence Forces and was told that there were none at that time. Shortly afterwards a priest a few years ahead of me was appointed to the Air Corps as chaplain so I knew that service in our own national forces was out for the foreseeable future. I then asked the bishop if I could make enquiries to the British and American military chaplaincy services and he said I could, but that there was no need to approach the Archbishop at such an early stage. The US forces wrote back and invited me to contact their chaplaincy service stationed with the US forces in England, but I also received a very nice letter from the senior chaplain in the British Army inviting me to fly over to see him. This was a fully paid for trip so I decided, with my bishop's blessing, to go ahead. I flew from Aldergrove in Belfast and met the chaplain at the airport. I had all the necessary documentation and the interview went very well. I had undergone a very stringent medical and after I had returned home I received a letter from the chaplaincy service requesting that I get the official sanction from my Archbishop in order for my application to go further.

I immediately contacted my bishop to inform him of this and

he told me he had mentioned this to the Archbishop and that I now had to go and request permission from the Archbishop to be released from the Archdiocese. I rang Archbishop's House and got an appointment to see the Archbishop. As the time drew closer I grew more and more nervous. My friends all thought it was a *fait accompli,* except for one priest who said there was no way the diocese would allow me to go after only two years' service. It was now August 1995. How right he was. I went to see the Archbishop and was given seven minutes of his time. As it turned out, my timing couldn't have been worse. It was just around now that the tidal wave of allegations of clerical abuse was beginning to break on the Archdiocese and the country. In the course of our brief chat, the Archbishop told me to give up 'wanting to play soldiers' and to be a good boy and go back to my parish. In those two sentences my career as an army chaplain perished. I think I was more hurt by the manner in which I was dismissed out of hand as 'wanting to play soldiers.' However, I was unaware of the volume of allegations that were crossing his desk at this particular time, so the desire of a young priest to do military chaplaincy overseas was most likely very low on his agenda, but a little more tact would have been appreciated.

I returned home to my parish, bitterly disappointed, and resumed my duties. To say that I felt completely undervalued by my Archbishop was an understatement and I believe that it was from now on the scales fell away from my eyes and I began to look deeply at everything that was going on in the church as a whole. I found it harder and harder to read out bishops' letters telling the people what to do and how to live their lives as I began to feel that what was issuing forth from the hierarchy was having less and less to do with the reality in which the faithful were living their lives. I also wondered what was I doing when I preached about the witness of people in Northern Ireland and received anonymous letters from a parishioner calling me a loyalist, and a few weeks later preaching about the area on which the church was built having been a training ground for the volunteers of 1916 and the same correspondent accusing me of being a republican. I found out who he was afterwards and made sure he knew that I was aware of his poisoned pen.

I went on holiday to friends in England in the September of that year in a very confused state. I had seen my dreams of chaplaincy dashed. I seemed to be in conflict with the official discipline of the church in a number of areas. I was working more and more with people whose lifestyles excluded them from the sacraments of the church according to official teaching. One couple were living together in a second or 'irregular union' and the daughter of the woman was making her First Holy Communion. The woman arrived at my door one night terribly upset as she had been told by a priest that she was not to come up for Communion at the ceremony as her lifestyle precluded her. She had explained to the priest about her circumstances and was treated in this way as a result of her honesty. I told her to come to me for Communion on the day and she and her partner did so. The other priest challenged me over this and I asked him if he knew whether or not all of the people he had given the sacrament to on the day were in a state of grace sufficient enough to receive Holy Communion? He agreed that he did not know and I asked him why then he would censure the woman in this way. 'Because she told me what her circumstances were.' I was sad for both the woman and the priest who were both suffering for their honesty.

My work with people in second unions seemed to be taking me further and further into uncharted waters but I could not turn my back on these people. I was also ministering to a number of gay people who loved their partners but also loved their church and were in agony as a result.

I also realised that I had developed feelings for a woman I had met through my ministry. When I returned from holiday I turned on the evening news to discover that a priest I had worked with in a neighbouring parish had just been accused of a number of sexual assaults on altar boys. If I had been confused before, I was really in turmoil now. To make matters worse, I found out that the woman I had feelings for also had feelings for me, so where did I go from here? It seemed that once the allegations had been made against my colleague, the flood gates were opened and every day more and more priests were being accused. The media delighted in using the term 'paedophile priest' and some members of the public tarred all priests with the same brush. The whole dreadful story of the Fr Brendan Smith case came out and then in the October another priest in our area was also accused. It was a very difficult time to be a priest and I think I made it harder on myself by becoming involved with the woman I was close to. We were both grown adults and went into the relationship with our eyes open, but it was doomed from the start as the pressure of such a relationship, given its clandestine nature, puts an impossible strain on the parties involved.

It was around November when I received a phone call one Saturday afternoon from my bishop. He asked me to go to a family in my area of pastoral care in the parish who were related to a priest in a neighbouring parish. I was told that he had died of a heart attack behind the wheel of his car and I was tasked with breaking the news to the family. I did so and thought no more about it. I knew the priest and had found him unfriendly and hard to deal with so it didn't pose a huge problem to me to go and break the news to the family. This makes me sound terribly callous but as I had no real relationship with the man, his death did not impact on me greatly – at least not yet.

I was on the early Sunday mass the next day and went and said the mass. The parish priest was in the sacristy when I came back in from the church and he was reading the morning paper. 'Have you seen the front page?' he asked me. I hadn't and nearly fainted when I saw a picture of the deceased priest under a banner headline which read: 'Priest found dead in gay sauna.' It seems that the priest had indeed suffered a heart attack but it had happened in the gay sauna club he frequented and not behind the wheel of his car as had been first reported. Some of his friends were attempting to move him to protect his modesty when somebody recognised the priest and contacted the media who went on a feeding frenzy. I was immediately accused by the family of trying to cover up what really happened but I only told them what I had been told. The next few days saw the clergy of the area being plagued by the media. Stories of the 'Deanery of Shame' and questions like 'Who is next?' were doing the rounds in the papers. The parishioners were dazed at the fact that two priests in the area had been accused of being child abusers and now another priest had died in a gay club – I use the term as used at the time and do not mean it in any offensive way. The funeral of the priest was held in the parish in which he had served and it was great to see the church absolutely packed with parishioners and priests – the media were in their hundreds outside and it was hard to be there but we had to be there. Many of the late priest's parishioners took the approach, 'Isn't it sad that he could only be himself in secret?' This shows the esteem in which this man was held by his parishioners.

With all this going on, I was more and more confused. I knew that what I was doing, being involved with someone, was wrong but found it hard to end things. Then I got a phone call from my bishop. It seems that my fellow priests in the parish had seen my 'friend' going in and out of the house and my own demeanour had led them to put two and two together, and they went to see the bishop about me. I went to see him and he asked me if I was in any kind of trouble? I said that I was and he asked me if I was involved with someone. I said 'Yes' and then his next words are so vivid in my mind.

Bishop: 'Is it a woman?'

Mark: 'Yes.'

Bishop: 'Is she over 18?'

Mark: 'Yes'.

Bishop: 'Thank God, at least you are normal!'

My only reaction to this statement was to laugh and he asked me what did I want to do. At this point I knew in my heart that the relationship was going nowhere but also knew that I needed time out from parish ministry to get back on track. I also felt that I could no longer work in the parish after being reported by the priests in the parish. I wished that they had come to me first instead of going to the bishop. Any trust or collegiality was now gone forever.

I agreed with the bishop that I would leave the parish the following June in the normal round of moves, but my parish priest decided that he wanted things sorted before he went on holiday and didn't want me in the parish with the forthcoming silver jubilee celebrations. So I was informed by the parish priest that I would be leaving the parish on 31 December. Merry Christmas, I don't think!

I was being moved to an apartment close to Archbishop's House and was allowed choose the venue for a short sabbatical course. The Archbishop did support me at this time and gave me all the space I needed to get back on track. A difficult Christmas ensued and my 'friend' and I parted company in January 1996. I think it was a huge relief for us all. My parents were very worried at this time but stood by me. When I think back, the way my move was handled was very poorly at a time when a priest disappearing from a parish usually meant that he was being accused of something serious. Clearly this did not concern my parish priest, a man I had thought to be a friend.

CHAPTER EIGHT

Here I stand; I can take no other course

I attended All Hallows College from January to May 1996 for the sabbatical course and went through a time of depression that I had never experienced either before or after, and I pray that I never go through anything like it again. I must acknowledge the friendship of a number of fellow clergy and religious on that course who helped me through the bad times, as well as the friendship and support of some friends from the Civil Defence. The greatest treasures God can give us are good friends, and these people restored my faith in others which had been sorely dented. I also attended regular counselling sessions with a priest of the Archdiocese who had been one of my lecturers in Clonliffe and he helped me talk things out. I still wanted to be a priest but had huge problems with the church as I had experienced it. I was also angry at the way I had been hounded out of my parish because I was involved with a woman, in light of the fact of how many priests who had had allegations of abuse made against them had been either protected or moved to another parish, free to continue on with their terrible crimes. I was beginning to wonder were the actions of a priest being involved with a woman deemed to be of greater gravity than the abuse of children by a cleric? This may seem like a petty comment but it is made as a result of what I have seen with my own eyes and experienced from other priests who have left, and indeed some who have stayed.

My course was drawing to a close and it was time for me to see the Archbishop about the way forward. I was not ready to go back into parochial ministry just yet and asked permission to return to my parish in London for the summer as I knew they had lost their curate and the parish priest and I had mused on what an ideal arrangement it would be for all of us. To my complete surprise, the Archbishop agreed with me and gave me his complete backing, provided I would be willing to be appointed in the September round of clerical changes.

So off I went to the east end of London to enjoy the happiest period of my ministry as a Roman Catholic priest. I became curate in the parish and really enjoyed once again the closeness of the Roman Catholic community in London. This was not just an Irish community but Catholics from all over the world. I was very busy with weddings, baptisms and funerals and in no time at all it was drawing close to the time for me to return to Ireland. I was very tempted to seek a transfer from the Dublin Archdiocese to work in the Brentwood Diocese but something stopped me from doing so.

I learned in early August 1996 that I was being appointed to the parish next door to my home parish. I thought that this was very odd but I had requested a south side appointment – just not that far south. Part of me wondered was I being sent to a place where being so well known – I had gone to school in this area – that I would be kept under so close a watch that I would not dream of becoming involved with a woman again.

Nevertheless, I was happy enough to be going to a place I knew well and again I knew both of the priests I would be working with and can say in all honesty that they redeemed my faith in my clerical colleagues. I took up my appointment in September 1996 and started out full of hopes for the future but with a nagging doubt – had I come back into ministry for the right reason? I was still uncomfortable with the institutional church. I still found it hard to read out the missives from Archbishop's House and I found myself more and more in conflict with some areas of official Roman Catholic teaching, particularly with regard to the treatment of people in second relationships. I had begun to conduct blessings for couples in these so-called 'second unions'. I found, and still find it hard to understand how the church can be so hard on people in second relationships. They are officially deemed 'irregular unions' and people in such unions are precluded from receiving Holy Communion. As I have shown earlier, I firmly believe that people deserve a second chance and saw the pain that this exclusion from the church caused many people in committed loving relationships. I was happy to say mass in a couple's home and allow them to exchange rings and commit themselves to each other. This ceremony had no legal standing but it meant a great deal to the couple and their families, and surely helping people to be happy was part of the reason I was ordained? I had begun to conduct these ceremonies very soon after my ordination as a priest.

As with all such clandestine practices, word leaked out and I was reprimanded in a roundabout way by an official from the church, even though other clergy were referring people to me for such ceremonies, which these priests would or could not perform themselves. I was growing more and more uncomfortable with what I saw was happening in the church – abuse scandals everywhere, priests and people leaving in great numbers and yet the rules and regulations were being imposed more and more strictly on the people all the time. I was also struggling in my own personal life as opportunities for relationships did present themselves at various times and I was flattered but was not in a good place at that time and found life to be very difficult in so many ways. People today may say that I was being deceitful to remain in the church with all of this turmoil, but I still felt a call to priesthood deep within my heart but was still trying to discover just what kind of priesthood it was that I was called to. Some people have been hurt along the way and it saddens me to think that I caused anybody pain, especially those who were close to me.

Not long after I started in my new parish I met the new Church of Ireland curate who had started a few months before me – he had been mistaken for me on a few occasions, much to the amusement of both of us. We had a number of long chats about our respective ministries and I liked what I heard about his ministry – it sounded very similar to my own and his theology sounded far more in line with my way of thinking than the official Roman Catholic training I had undergone. One evening he commented that I should just be honest and declare myself to be an Anglican because the more he had got to know me the more he realised just how un-Roman Catholic I really was. His comment really threw me but it certainly gave me cause for thought and a few broken nights sleep ensued.

Not long after this the President of Ireland attended a Holy Communion service in Christchurch Cathedral in Dublin and received the sacrament during the service. This was equally praised and condemned in the days following the service. The Roman Catholic Archbishop condemned the President for her actions and went on to refer to a Roman Catholic partaking in the Anglican Eucharist as a 'sham'. I spoke out in my Sunday sermon in defence of the President and received huge support from my parishioners – one parishioner attacked me for defending what he deemed the 'indefensible actions of our leader' and said he would never receive Holy Communion from me again – which he didn't.

After much soul searching I finally asked my colleague in the Church of Ireland parish to sound out as to whether or not the Anglican Archbishop of Dublin would meet with me. I had met him at my friend's ordination to the priesthood and he had seemed taken aback when he heard that I had administered Holy Communion in the Anglican Church at my friend's first mass. He expressed a hope that I would not get into trouble with my own church authorities for not only receiving Communion in an Anglican church but also administering it too. Funnily enough, I never heard any official comment about this incident. The Archbishop agreed to meet me and a date was set for me to go and see him at See House, the official residence of the Archbishop.

I still wasn't sure what I was going to say to him and also wondered should I wear clerical garb or not. The day dawned for the meeting and I decided to dress as a priest because I reasoned that more would be thought of me being seen there in lay dress as opposed to clerical dress so, thus attired, I arrived for my meeting with five minutes to spare. An abiding memory of the meeting is the burst of barking from the Archbishop's dogs when I rang the doorbell. When the Archbishop answered the door himself – an unheard of event in Drumcondra – he referred to the dogs as his *aides-de-camps*, to which I answered that the Catholic Archbishop had two priests for the same role. The Archbishop roared with laughter and I immediately felt at ease and welcome.

The Archbishop was very friendly and open in the meeting and I asked him, after a short time, about the possibility of me becoming an Anglican. Despite opinions expressed in the past about him by those who clearly did not know him, I found the him to be a highly intuitive and deeply insightful man. He immediately asked me if I wanted to become an Anglican or an Anglican priest. By asking me such a direct question, he spared me much prevarication and I asked him if I could become an Anglican priest. It was then I learned that my two Church of Ireland colleagues had filled the Archbishop in about me. He asked me a lot of straight questions about why I wanted to leave the Roman Catholic Church and join the Church of Ireland. I answered as best I could. Some could say that I had been angry with the Roman Catholic Archbishop for refusing to allow me to become an army chaplain – if this was the case, why was I still in active ministry? Some could say that I was doing this to marry – if this was the case, why didn't I just leave and find a job? This was at a time when the economy was improving and career paths were opening in many fields. I genuinely felt, and still feel, that I was called to minister as a priest but not as a Roman Catholic one. I always felt confident that I was good at what I did in ministry, but that my ministry was more and more distanced from official Roman Catholic teaching as time went on.

After a meeting that lasted an hour and a half, the Archbishop asked me if I was willing to meet with some people so that he could get their opinion of me. I readily agreed to this and went away feeling drained and at the same time elated.

The following month the Archbishop asked me to go and meet the Principal and Vice Principal of the Church of Ireland Theological College. Priests transferring from other churches to the Church of Ireland had in the past been asked to attend St Deniol's Library in North Wales for a year of study. However, the House of Bishops had felt that priests in this situation needed to get to know the clergy they would minister with, so it was decided that from now on transferring clergy would spend a year at the Theological College and attend a certain number of lectures both there and in Trinity College. The two clergy from the Theological College were friendly and asked me about my educational qualifications and the course of studies I had undertaken in Clonliffe, in order for them to draw up a course to suit my needs. This was the first inkling that all was going well. I thank God every day that I completed the Bachelor of Divinity Degree in Holy Cross College as it has certainly opened many doors to me. I can't say that my first impression of the Theological College was all that favourable, but this was to change. I think it was more the thoughts of going back to college life than any real reflection on Braemor Park.

All during this process I was still ministering as a priest in my parish. I know that some reading this will ask was I not being a hypocrite by ministering whilst planning to leave. I can honestly say that I gave everything I could to the people in my parish and tried – successfully, I hope – not to allow my personal turmoil to interfere in my ministry. I had decided early on in this process that if I was going to leave, I would do it for the right reasons and be as sure as I possibly could be when I did leave.

Personal situations arose which made my decision all the easier but more about that later. I really came to an important turning point at Christmas 1996 when I experienced a venomous phone call from a person who attacked me for closing the church before her family had received confession. Before this call I had been wrestling with my conscience about leaving – what would my family and friends think, who would I hurt, would I be wanted and welcomed into the Church of Ireland? All valid questions and each had to be dealt with in turn. I also wondered if this was just a reaction to all of the abuse stories in the church and the way I had seen priests treated when their involvement with women had been revealed.

I returned to the presbytery after closing up the church for an hour or so before the children's Christmas play. I had made sure that the two other priests, who had been hearing confessions all afternoon, had got away to get something to eat as a long night was ahead. The phone was ringing as I walked in and I answered it to the words, 'Who the f##king hell do you think you are?' The 'lady' then proceeded to attack me because her daughter had gone off to college down the country for Christmas examinations and would not get a chance for confession before Christmas. I asked the lady if there were no priests where her daughter studied – add fuel to the fire, why don't you Mark?' – Clearly the lady didn't appreciate the remark and started another tirade of abuse. I thanked her for the call and wished her a blessed and peaceful Christmas and put the phone down. I just said to myself that God really must still want me to be a priest if I was happy to continue to minister to people even if they wanted to use me as a sounding board for their anger. I do think that the woman wanted to make sure her children attended confession with her to see that they did, as she was concerned that they wouldn't on their own and this sacrament was clearly very important to her. I had calmed down sufficiently by supper time to amuse my colleagues with the story, but it really struck a chord deep within me. Organised religion can bring out both the best and worst in people at times. Believe it or not, the lady did ring in the New Year to apologise for speaking to me in the way she did and I accepted her apology but asked her to think about the real reason for her anger on the day. I never did find out who she was but hope that she is calmer and happier at Christmas since.

In the summer of 1997 I was asked to meet two Church of Ireland bishops at See House for a final interview. I would receive the final decision from the Archbishop after this meeting. During the course of this meeting I was asked a lot of questions about my reasons for wanting to leave and one sticks in my mind: 'Do you think you will marry?' I answered this question by asking the bishop if he had known for sure that he would marry? This raised a smile and the bishop agreed that mine was a fair point. The other bishop pointed out to me that I wasn't leaving the Catholic family but just joining another branch of it, and that comment has stuck with me ever since.

Not long after this meeting, the Archbishop contacted me and said that he was happy for me to join the Anglican Church. I thanked him for the offer but told him that I intended to finish out the year in my parish as I wanted to be absolutely sure that I was doing the right thing. I still wonder if that was the wisest or stupidest decision of my life. This was to be the hardest period I experienced in ministry but I can honestly say that, when I left in July 1998, I knew that I was doing it for the right reasons and I had no regrets.

CHAPTER NINE

Lorraine and Adieu

But I am jumping ahead a year. My decision to remain for a further period is a decision I have questioned many times since taking it. Should I have gone once I had been accepted? Should I have taken a year out from everything to get myself ready for what lay ahead? I can never answer any of those questions sufficiently well for myself or anybody else, but I do know I served the people of the parish as best I could.

It was towards the end of the summer of 1997 that I met the woman who was to become my wife. One of my Church of Ireland cousins was marrying her partner of many years in the church where I was curate, as her partner was Roman Catholic. I was always in and out of her house as her mum worked with me in one of the parish schools. So I arrived in one Sunday morning between masses to meet a sea of corpses all over the place – it was the morning after the hen night. I chatted to those who were conscious and one woman caught my eye very quickly. I was not looking for anybody as I was an emotional mess at this time and was fit company for neither man nor beast. Besides, I had enough going on without an added complication to an already complicated situation.

In spite of all of this, a few weeks later at the wedding rehearsal Lorraine and I had a chance to chat and we both seemed to 'click' with each other very quickly. We spent a lot of time together at the wedding and we arranged to meet after Lorraine returned from holiday at the end of the month.

We met up as arranged and we had a long chat about how we felt about each other and what was ahead. I explained to

Lorraine what I was planning to do and that maybe we had a chance of a future together once I had left the Roman Catholic Church. To my complete surprise, Lorraine agreed that she thought we had a future too and we took the first steps on a path that would lead to marriage and two wonderful children. This period in our life was not easy because the relationship had to be a hidden one, and that places an incredible strain on the couple concerned. The fact that Lorraine moved to County Tipperary shortly after we started seeing each other was both a plus and a minus. Anyone who has been in a long distance relationship will know the strain of being apart, but it also made things a lot less pressured being so far away from family and work mates. Was I deceitful engaging in a relationship before I had left? I was. How can I say otherwise, but at that point I had already left internally long before I physically left.

So, by now I had sought out the Church of Ireland, I had applied and been accepted to become a clergyman in that church and I had met and fallen in love with a wonderful woman. There were two more hurdles to cross before I could finally leave the Roman Catholic Church. I had to resign from the ministerial priesthood – once a priest, always a priest – and break the news to my parents. I knew how the Archbishop of the day viewed the reformed churches, so I was under no illusion as to how he would react to one of his priests resigning from 'Holy Mother Church'. Given the way I had been treated by the Archbishop when I had applied to join the British Army, I felt that the he only needed to know that I was leaving. What I did afterwards was my concern. This may appear odd but given the nature of my future plans, I knew that I would be harangued by an Archbishop who was already under huge pressure given what was going on in the rest of the Archdiocese and the Roman Catholic Church in Ireland. Me breaking the news of what I intended to do would have been the final straw at that time, I imagine.

I contacted Archbishop's house and requested a meeting

with the Archbishop. As he had been very direct to me in the past, and in fairness, kind to me at times, I immediately told him that I wanted to resign from the ministry. He was naturally saddened that I wanted to do this and asked me to meet with a number of priests to talk it over. I did this but returned for the next meeting still intent on leaving. What really shocked me at this next meeting was how prepared the Archbishop was to grant me any appointment of my choice, including a military chaplaincy post. This both angered and saddened me. Was I only being offered this in a vain attempt to make me change my mind? Did he know me so little that he thought this was still me sulking three years later? I declined the offers and the Archbishop told me to go to the head of finance to sort out my affairs but also to go and see a priest about whether I wanted to be laicised or not. I did this but informed the priest that I did not want to be laicised as the Pope generally did not grant laicisation and it was not an issue for me. After these meetings I went back to see the Archbishop one last time and he came across as a man who was sad but also angry. I was to cease working in my parish on 5 July and my faculties to say mass and administer the sacraments in the Archdiocese would be revoked the same day.

I then had to go and inform my parents that I was leaving the parish. I still couldn't bring myself to tell them that I was leaving the Roman Catholic Church as well. I was curate in the neighbouring parish, related to many people in the area and was a popular priest amongst the people as I ministered to everybody, irrespective of who or what they were. I finally went to see my parents and told them that I was leaving the parish to take time out and do some studies. I think they had an idea I was leaving but they played along with what I was telling them. I had decided to go over to England for a month just to settle down and then come back and break the news to them. I wrote a letter to the Archbishop informing him of what I was intending to do as I felt that I owed him the courtesy of hearing it from me first. I should have told my parents at the same time but didn't and this is something I regret. I handled this part of the whole process very badly.

I had planned to go to England to sort myself out. I stayed with my aunt and uncle, both of whom were Anglican – my maternal uncle came to Anglicanism later in life and I chatted to him a lot in those weeks to learn a little bit more about this 'tradition' I was joining. I spent a month in England, two weeks on my own and the last two weeks with Lorraine. This was a good time for us as it gave us time to be a couple openly for the first time. This may seem funny to many reading this but to be able to be openly affectionate in public is something unknown to a Roman Catholic cleric. This was the calm before the storm.

When I returned to Ireland the rumour mill was hard at work and I soon had to tell my father what I was doing. This came as a huge blow to him, and can you imagine what it must have been like for him? Here was his only son, the popular priest not only leaving the priesthood but also leaving the church he was raised in. It is a credit to my father's love for me that we have come through all of this and are still close today. My mother was a rock in this process as she had to support me and my father, both of us at totally opposite points on the compass for some time.

It would be pointless for me to go into detail as to what was said between my father and me, but suffice it to say that in August 1998 I thought that my relationship with my father was irreparably damaged. Lorraine was my constant support at this time and my mother was caught between my father and myself.

The main priority for me at this time was to get myself emotionally ready to enter the Church of Ireland Theological College at the end of September for the year long course I had agreed to take part in. I did not know much of what was ahead of me but, on the other hand, neither did the staff of the college. The files of the two 'former Roman clergy', as we were being referred to, were only given to the wider college staff the week before we entered. I had only learned a few weeks before I entered that there was another former Roman Catholic priest entering the college at the same time as I was.

CHAPTER TEN

All change please!

Lorraine helped me move into my room in the college, on the third floor, and we happened to look out of the window to see another couple walking along holding hands. This couple were soon to become our closest clergy friends. Little did I know at the time that I was looking down at a fellow traveller – another former Roman Catholic priest searching for a spiritual and ministerial home within the Church of Ireland. This was a very different start to a stay in a religious house than in 1986 when my mother helped make my bed and left me a bag of goodies to keep me going. This time my fiancée helped me move in and held my hand at the welcome tea in the dining room. What a difference twelve years can make. That was the amount of time I had spent within the Roman Catholic system as a student and cleric. What was ahead? What sort of welcome would I receive? I would soon find out.

My first memorable incident in the college was meeting a First Year student who made a point of telling me that his father had a major problem with what I was doing. Never short of an answer, I responded by saying that my father had a problem with it too so his father would have to look after himself. The same student also asked me what a renowned Protestant theologian would have to say about me not being re-ordained. (The Anglican Church recognises the validity of the holy orders within the Roman Catholic Church – the Roman Catholic Church however does not repay the compliment.) I answered him by saying, 'Not much, seeing as he is dead!' Eventually this young man recognised that I had a genuine desire to be an Anglican and one day even went so far as to say that I was more 'Protestant' than many of the students within the college. Praise indeed! This was my first real experience of the tensions that exist within the members of the Anglican Church that are covered by the term 'Churchmanship'. As a former 'Roman' I was familiar with conservative, middle of the road and liberal clergy. Now I was exposed to terms like high, low, middle of the road, Anglo-Catholic, evangelical, saved, reformed, born again and many more. It was immediately presumed that because I had been a Roman Catholic that I would be of a high church persuasion – meaning that I was into a very Catholic form of worship, similar in many ways to traditional Roman Catholic liturgy. It came as quite a shock to many within the college that I had more in common with the low/evangelical wing of the church – a form of worship more in keeping with the founding fathers of the Reformation – a simpler, more scripturally-based form of worship with none of the trappings of high worship. This was more in keeping with how I had been as a Roman Catholic priest and I felt very much at home with an unadorned Communion Table, no candles and a straight forward prayerful service. This still comes as a shock to some of my colleagues, and one of my good friends and clergy neighbours in my current diocese reckons I get more Protestant as the years go on.

Life in the college was not as pressurised for the two former Romans as it was for the other ordinands as they were preparing for final examinations whereas we were attending a number of lectures with no examinations at the end. We entered in late September 1998 and in the first week of October my colleague and I were licensed to minister in the parishes where we were assigned as 'Student Reader'. I was truly blessed with the parish I was appointed to and the rector opened his heart and his home to me and became, and still is, one of my closest friends and advisors. We spent more time working in the parishes we had been assigned than the amount of time we spent in the classroom and if I am honest, whilst the fellowship in the college was good, and getting to know future colleagues was invaluable, it may have been of more benefit for us to have been placed in a parish full-time and attended the college when we had lectures. However, it would be hard to know what system would have worked better as the ideal seminary system did not and does not exist and each seminary/theological college has its strengths and weaknesses. I did enjoy the fact that the ordinands were treated as adults. As Roman Catholic seminarians we were treated as adolescents regardless whether one was a school leaver or an older entrant. The attitude was 'Will I be ordained?' whereas the attitude in the Church of Ireland system is 'Will I go forward for ordination?' This, in my own opinion, is a far healthier approach as the decision to go forward should be a personal one and not just if one is allowed to do so.

I attended many of the various classes that were taking place in the college and discovered that I had already covered much of what the course work entailed, but the lectures that were of great interest were those dealing with Anglican history and Anglican liturgy. It may surprise some readers that I was now celebrating Anglican services whilst having very little knowledge of the liturgical or historical tradition or basis from which they came. As a result I was on a very steep learning curve but this was good because it helped me to take my mind off the personal upset I was going through. My relationship with Lorraine was going from strength to strength and I lived for Friday afternoon when I could go to spend some of the weekend with this wonderful woman.

My family relationships, however, were in a poor state. My father and I were not speaking at all and my poor mother was caught in between two peas in a pod for my father and I have identical temperaments. We love each other dearly but were both very angry with each other at this time – Dad was angry at me for my actions and I was angry at him for his reactions. Many people got caught in the fall-out and have the sense today not to tease either of us about that time. I came to the conclusion that each time I spoke to my father we both got upset so I decided – rightly or wrongly – to stop talking to him after Christmas 1998. I just had to have time to clear my head and in hindsight we both needed the space, but it is a period that neither of us can ever get back and I regret that.

From December 1998 onwards the long awaited 'curacy rounds' loomed over the horizon. As a Roman Catholic priest, I was used to being told where I was being appointed to and accepting the position with no say whatsoever. The system in the Church of Ireland is far different. In every year, there are a certain number of ordinands approaching ordination as deacons. There are also a number of parishes that are looking for a curate to assist the rector in his/her ministry. The names of the ordinands are distributed to the clergy along with CVs, and parish profiles are distributed to the ordinands. A rector can indicate to the college the ordinands that he/she would like to meet for interview and the ordinand can do the same. I was interested in a number of parishes, all of which were within the Republic of Ireland as I had been advised that someone with my background would have to have proved himself within the Church of Ireland before considering working in Northern Ireland. I have to be honest and say that I still wonder at how good or bad this advice was and would love to have had an opportunity to work in the north. Five rectors indicated an interest in meeting with me, two of whom were in Northern Ireland, so the last week of my Christmas holidays were spent visiting four of the rectors for interview. The fifth rector met the interviewees in Dublin as so many had indicated an interest in his parish. After the interviews had taken place, the ordinand had to express his/her preference in order 1, 2 and 3 and so did the rector. Then we had to wait. One rector was very keen for me to come to his parish and I expressed reluctance to work in Dublin again, having served as a Roman Catholic priest in Dublin too. I feared that it would be awkward and also unfair to many people if I came back to Dublin so soon, but I was proved wrong on both counts.

The day of the announcement came and neither of the former Romans 'got' a parish in the first round but I was asked to reconsider working in Dublin again which I did and I was nominated as curate assistant of Monkstown, County Dublin. My fellow traveller was also approached to work in Dublin.

So, the year rolled on, with plans for our wedding going well and the prospect of making history – curate of the Roman Catholic Archdiocese of Dublin and curate assistant of the Church of Ireland Archdiocese of Dublin and Glendalough. Relations at home still were not good but I was hopeful that reconciliation would be reached before our wedding day in October 1999. Life was busy as in May 1999 I began my ministry in my new parish. Given my experience as a priest, it was agreed that I would serve a two year period as a curate assistant and after that I would be allowed to look for a position as a rector. Getting used to parish life was challenging, as was planning for the wedding and the fact that Lorraine was still living in Kilkenny whilst I was living in Dublin. Absence really does make the heart grow fonder.

My duties involved taking services, parish visitation, hospital visits, sick calls and all the usual round of duties for a priest. Given that I was serving within a short car drive from my old parishes in both directions, it was inevitable for me to meet many former parishioners from time to time. I was deeply touched at how supportive so many of them were and those who weren't I met with grace and moved on (but it did hurt for a time). Two incidents during this time spring to mind. I was walking along the street in the parish one day when I spotted one of my classmates from my Roman Catholic seminary. He spotted me, I am sure, because he crossed the street in order not to have to acknowledge me. Sadly, he was not the only member of my ordination class to ignore my existence. I have never heard from any of my serving classmates since I left the Roman Catholic Church. The other incident shows how true the old saying 'What goes around comes around' really is. You may remember that I mentioned a man attacking me for defending President McAleese's decision to receive Holy Communion in an Anglican Cathedral. I was visiting a Dublin hospital in 2000 and met this man's wife who was visiting him in hospital. The man was quite ill and hadn't seen a priest for a number of days. His wife asked me to come in and pray with him which I did. The man never spoke – indeed I don't think he could at that stage – but his eyes spoke volumes: 'Of all the priests, she found you.' I prayed for them both and blessed the man and went home firmly convinced that God has a way of closing old wounds in a very unusual way.

The date of our marriage was fast approaching and everything was falling into place – the church was booked (eventually), the hotel, invitations chosen and all the other jobs associated with the big day. My colleague from the theological college was going to marry us and really saved the day as the priest in charge of where we married was unhappy at the prospect of a former Roman Catholic priest marrying in 'his' cathedral lest it offend the Roman Catholic Archbishop. Sadly the compliment was not returned as Roman Catholic/Church of Ireland relations were further strained by unfortunate comments by the Roman Catholic Archbishop about the Anglican Archbishop. I do wish the priest had voiced his unease to me but he never did. In testimony to the pastoral care of his priests, the Archbishop intervened and our marriage went ahead in a most beautiful setting. Thankfully the Archbishop could see me for what I was – a priest of the Church of Ireland, not just a former Roman Catholic priest working in the Church of Ireland.

A far more worrying development had arisen that drove that minor hiccup well out of my mind. My mother rang me and told me that my father had decided not to attend our wedding. I had been in contact with my parents again and relations were polite albeit strained, but I really hoped that Dad would come to the wedding. Sadly he had made up his mind and would not budge. I really believed right up to the day before our wedding that he would change his mind but he didn't and I met with him the day before we married and we spoke together alone. What we said remains between us and always will, but suffice it to say that I went to the cathedral on the day of my marriage with my father's blessing in my heart.

I have conducted a large number of weddings during my ministry, many of which were the weddings of friends. I never appreciated just how nerve wracking an experience a wedding day can be for the bride and groom. I know that I certainly was a very nervous groom when I arrived for the ceremony. I had given couples plenty of advice in the past about keeping calm, pacing themselves and making the most of their time together before the big day, but this was advice given from what I had observed about weddings. I had never appreciated just how much work goes into a wedding day. The ceremony, the reception, the dreaded table plan, the dresses, the suits, the flowers and on and on. It is no wonder that so many couples arrive at their wedding day completely exhausted. As a single priest I had often expressed the view that there was an awful lot of fuss attached to weddings that is unnecessary, but having prepared for our own wedding, I can now see how much pressure is exerted by society and in some cases family about how a wedding should turn out. Does the fact that I am married make me a better priest to conduct a wedding ceremony? Perhaps it does and perhaps it doesn't, but I can certainly identify with the pressures that the couples face and can pass on my own experience of the problems that can be faced, but many single priests are equally adept at marriage ceremonies as are married clergy.

I arrived at the cathedral very early for the ceremony –

what's new? – I always arrive early at church. This drives Lorraine mad but it is a personal idiosyncrasy that I have – a terrible fear of being late for church. Guests were already arriving and it was great to see so many family members and friends turning up for the marriage. However, as glad as I was to see our guests, the only person I needed to see was Lorraine. We had joked about her being the traditional few minutes late on the evening of the rehearsal but despite Friday lunchtime traffic in the city centre, Lorraine arrived early for the ceremony, before some of the guests in fact. I sat at the head of the church and was relieved when the entrance music started. My bride looked beautiful but I wondered why my future father-in-law looked so tearful. It seems he was so overcome at the occasion that he started to cry as they came up the church – this reflects how much John loves his family. Much of the ceremony passed in a blur but I remember clearly our vows and it meant so much that my fellow traveller Dermot conducted our marriage ceremony – who better? After we had become husband and wife we went through the usual round of photographs and our friend Charley Sharkey did us proud with a wonderful record of the day.

After the ceremony we headed off to the Stand House Hotel on the Curragh for our reception but I asked our driver – another friend, Eddie – to stop at a service station on the Naas road to get sandwiches as neither of us had eaten breakfast, so high was our level of anxiety. I got some sandwiches for the three of us and queued up. The girl at the counter looked up and saw a very over dressed customer. 'Off to a wedding then are you?' she asked me. 'Yes I am actually – my wedding.' Yeah right.' 'No, I am – look out at the wedding car!' She looked out and saw the wedding car complete with bride and wished me well, but she still charged me for the sandwiches though!

We had a wonderful time at the hotel and everybody enjoyed a wonderful meal and great fun at the reception. A long late night ensued and many of the guests stayed in the hotel. There was great 'craic' at the breakfast table the next day. After a lovely weekend we flew off on honeymoon on the Sunday, bound for Mexico and the first chapter in the new book of our life together.

We returned from honeymoon and settled back into the reality of married life. Lorraine went to work for a company in Dublin and I continued to work as a curate. I had always envied the working relationship that was evident between the rector and his/her curate in the parish where I had served as a Roman Catholic priest. In my own limited experience, Roman Catholic priests very often worked on their own, meeting perhaps once or twice a week and being largely responsible for their own area of responsibility. From the outside looking in, it appeared that there was far more support in the Church of Ireland system. However, from my own experience I soon learned that a Church of Ireland curate assistant has very little autonomy and is in a parish to effectively shadow the rector, who is really completing the training started by the college. One point should be made clear: as a Roman Catholic curate you start in a parish as a fully ordained priest whereas in the Church of Ireland you start in a parish as a fully ordained deacon and priesthood follows a year later. There are pluses and minuses in both systems but if a curate is lucky enough to spend time with a thoughtful and experienced rector, it will stand them in great stead in the future. I was a different kettle of fish for my rector as he was landed with someone who had been an ordained cleric for seven years and one who had a lot of baggage. It is a testimony to his character that he agreed to have me as a curate at all, as I was bruised and touchy to say the least. I had come out of a process of leaving one church and joining another and now this decision was truly going to be put to the test when I began working in an Anglican parish.

Whilst I may have found the system a little hard to get used to *vis-à-vis* the rector-curate working relationship, I found (and continue to find) that denominational differences matter little when a person needs someone to talk to or needs support in a time of crisis. I found my time as a curate rewarding, challenging, infuriating, draining and eye opening. By the winter of 2000 my time was drawing to a close and I spoke to the Archbishop about permission to start looking for parishes that were looking for a rector. I also discussed this with my rector whose comment was, 'You're in a fierce hurry to be a rector. Enjoy the peace of being a curate while you can. A curate will always be the golden haired boy whereas the buck stops with the rector.' How right he was – and still is! (It was also around this time that I took the mad step of writing a book on military awards. I had been looking for a book about a particular area in which I was interested and asked a fellow collector if he know of a book on the subject and he said, 'No, so why don't you write one?' I laughed but the idea began to grow and as a result in 2001 I published my first book, with a second in 2005. No one has been more surprised about this than me!)

I had heard from other curates and rectors the excitement they felt when parochial nominators rang them to ask them to come for interview. I was soon to experience this myself. I scanned the back of the church paper every week to see what parishes were vacant and wrote off for a number of profiles. A parish in Dublin was looking for a rector and I was very disappointed when I wasn't approached for interview – the naïvety of youth! My turn would come soon enough. Seemingly the list of curates who were eligible for a move had been made known to the dioceses and my name was on the list. I was at home one Friday not long before Christmas and the phone rang. I was pretty tired and dreaded the thought of getting called out again on a miserable day. However, the person on the other end of the phone was a nominator from a parish in another diocese and was inviting me for interview. I was thrilled, and then the phone rang again and it was a nominator from another group of parishes also inviting me for interview. Before you think I must have been a wonder-curate, let me explain the system. In a parish group with four parishes, one person from each parish is appointed as parochial nominator and they meet with the Archdeacon and diocesan nominators when a parish becomes vacant. A brain storming session ensues and names are thrown out of people who may be a good choice or not, and one unfortunate gets the job of ringing the various individuals. It is often the case that out of ten names only one or two may actually come to meet the nominators. Meeting the nominators allows the cleric and his/her partner to see the parish, churches, rectory, and schools and so on. This can involve a whole day, depending on the size of the parochial group and the amount of questions both 'sides' may or may not have. Both sides go away and have a think about the process and if both continue to be interested, the candidate's name goes to the bishop and diocesan nominators to be considered at a meeting with the parochial nominators. If this candidate gets the approval of the entire board of nomination, then the bishop will contact the candidate and offer the parochial group to them. This is a much fairer system than the system I was used to in the Roman Catholic Church, but it is far from perfect.

I have jumped ahead. I had now been approached by two parochial groups in the same diocese and I had also asked for the profile of another group in the same diocese. I now had three parishes to consider, or so I thought. I was then approached by a parochial group in the Dublin diocese as well.

Lorraine and I decided to go and have a look at the parishes ourselves with no nominators around. It meant that we would have some idea of what the areas were like, so one Saturday early in January 2001 we headed off to the four groups that were on the table. A long day ensued with much food for thought and by the end of the day we had a fair idea of what group we would like to work in, if we were successful in interview. I contacted the Archdeacon of the diocese and indicated my interest in one parish group in particular and the wheels began to move. Lorraine and I were invited to meet the nominators at the rectory and we all had a good chat about the group and our hopes and expectations. Then we went on a tour of the four churches. At the end of the day Lorraine and I were happy with what we had seen and after another chat with the nominators, Lorraine and I decided to put our names forward for consideration. At this point I contacted the other groups that had called me for interview to let them know that I was in advanced talks with another group, out of fairness to them as they may have wanted to talk to other people until I knew what was happening. Maybe I was putting all my eggs in one basket but these people had been very kind to invite me for interview and I didn't want to repay their kindness by wasting their time.

I was invited by the bishop to meet with him for lunch one day in February and then to meet the diocesan nominators afterwards. I was very impressed at the reception I received from the bishop and we chatted about the parochial group and the future, as well as my experience to date. I then met the diocesan nominators and I am very grateful to them all for being so kind to me – something I now repay in full as a diocesan nominator myself. After this meeting I returned home, conscious of the fact that the bishop, parochial and diocesan nominators were meeting to make a decision. I was halfway home when my mobile rang and the bishop asked me to pull in. I was convinced that the parish had gone to someone else, but he offered it to me. I was elated but the bishop told me to go home and talk to Lorraine about it. Wise words indeed. Lorraine and I decided to accept the offer and I told my rector who was most unhappy at the prospect of losing his curate, but after some awkward moments he gave me his blessing to take the parish.

I contacted the bishop and informed him that I was happy to become rector-elect of the Gorey group of parishes. I then had to tender my notice to my rector and the Archbishop. I also informed the other three parishes that I was now nominated as rector of a parish group and wished them well in their search for a rector. The date for my institution as rector was set for the end of May 2001 and I now faced into the prospect of running a group of parishes on my own.

I now entered into uncharted waters as I was working out my notice, sorting out removal firms, assisting the parish glebe wardens with the renovations of the rectory, picking the brains of any rectors I knew about the pitfalls of starting out in a parish for the first time and also helping Lorraine come to terms with the prospect of leaving Dublin. Even though we were living in a small terraced house it was amazing how much stuff had been gathered up by us in so short a time. We also had to think about buying new furniture and all the other items that were needed. I was also learning about the area I was going to work in but couldn't visit much as the foot and mouth crisis was in full flow and moving around the country was severely restricted at that time.

The rectory slowly began to take shape and the parishes were very kind in agreeing to all that we asked in relation to renovations on the house. We were invited to a dinner party in the rectory of the neighbouring parish and it was there that I met the staff of the primary school that I was to become chairperson of.

It was shortly afterwards that we learned that we would be parents for the first time in the January of 2002. It is amazing the lengths a woman will go to in order to avoid lifting boxes, isn't it? 2001 was a remarkable year – I was going to be a father for the first time and I was also going to be a rector for the first time as well.

The run up to my leaving my parish for pastures new seemed to go in a blur of moving, decorating, choosing hymns for the service and the initial sessions of ante natal classes. Life was very busy and in no time at all the day of my institution as rector of Gorey arrived. The service was scheduled for the evening time and it was nice to wander around Gorey one last time as an anonymous figure. Lorraine and some of the family walked up to the church with me and we were amazed at the huge number of people who had gathered for the service. I was touched to see so many family and friends at the service and to see that so many colleagues had made the effort to be there. Prior to the service I had to sign the declarations and swear loyalty to the bishop and his successors and then the entrance procession formed up and very soon I was going through the beautiful ritual of becoming the incumbent of Gorey group of parishes. One moment sticks in my mind: my father receiving Holy Communion from the bishop – that spoke volumes to me of how far we had all come in such a short period of time, and this journey together has gone from strength to strength.

Once the institution was over I was then rector of the Gorey group of parishes. In my ministry to date I had always worked with at least one other priest and in a parish unit of no more than two churches. Now I was rector/parish priest of a group of parishes with four churches, a wide area of responsibility and I was the lead priest with a non-stipendiary colleague – a priest who works in his/her own job during the week and ministers in a parish at least one day a week and on a Sunday – and a diocesan reader and a parish reader. A diocesan reader is a person who is licensed and trained to conduct non-Holy Communion services in a diocese and a parish reader is licensed and trained to do the same in a parish group. This was a totally new experience for me and I was daunted by the prospect, but I was lucky to have the advice of colleagues who had been rectors longer than I was. I must say that my new parishioners were very kind to me and allowed me to make many mistakes in the first year – perhaps they think I still am years later, and we are all still getting used to each other.

Life has changed much since I began to minister here in Gorey. We have two beautiful sons, Luke and Daniel; we are more settled here now than ever before and I find that the longer you minister in a place the more effective you can become. Gorey has changed much in the past six years and I wonder how much Gorey and I will change together in the years ahead.

Do I have regrets? If I am totally honest with myself, there are things I would have done differently in some areas of my life but I do not regret my decision in any way. I have lost some friends and gained new ones but my experiences at my recent school re-union made me realise that what I have done has been received well by many of my peers and made little or no impact on others. What has happened to me over the last number of years has made me a far better person, changed collar and all.

People often ask me two recurring questions. The first is what do I consider myself to be? I am, I hope, a Christian first and an Anglican second. I also consider myself to be a catholic, a member of the universal Christian church. The second question still upsets me as I am often asked if I hate the Roman Catholic Church. I presume that this is asked in light of my experiences both before and after I left the active Roman Catholic ministry. My answer is the same today as it always has been. I was born and raised as a member of the Roman Catholic Church. It is as much part of me as my brown eyes or grey hair. I have issues with certain parts of the institutional church and I have a differ-ent theological understanding of some doctrines of the faith, but I was a Roman Catholic, an ordained priest of that church, and that can never change and nor should it. I am now a member of another branch of the 'catholic' family, to quote a well-known bishop of the Church of Ireland. There are many aspects of my birth church that I still hold in deep affection but there is much in the teachings of the church of my choosing that I find more in keeping with the kind of person that I am and am becoming. I am a Christian, as I said earlier, and it is incompatible with Christian living and doctrine (but sadly very often not in prac-tice) to hate or be intolerant of any religion, even those that are